What do you do when...

- Your prayers for healing go unanswered?
- You are told your prayers failed because you are harboring sin?
- Your marriage suddenly goes sour?
- Your finances are a mess?
- You "claim it," but don't get it?

Is it really because you have "hidden sins" or have made a "negative confession?" Do you really *need* that guilt in a time of trouble? Isn't it possible that there are times you simply have to accept certain events as being part of God's plan — even if you can't see the reason why? In GOD'S IN CHARGE HERE, Harold Hill admits to his own prayer failures and says there is comfort to be found in admitting that you *can't* fix everything — and shouldn't feel you *must* — because GOD'S IN CHARGE HERE, not you.

God's In Charge Here

Harold Hill
with Irene Burk Harrell

**Power
Books**

Fleming H. Revell Company
Old Tappan, New Jersey

Library of Congress Cataloging in Publication Data

Hill, Harold, date
    God's in charge here.

    (Power books)
    1. Resignation. 2. Trust in God. I. Harrell, Irene
Burk. II. Title.
BV4647.R4H44 1982   248.4   81-17763
ISBN 0-8007-5078-0   AACR2

TO
all the folks
who have suffered with me
through the many agonies
I haven't confessed till now

Contents

God's In Charge Here

1

How to Let God *Be* God

Warning!

This book may not be for you. . . .

Maybe you'd be uncomfortable hearing about the failures and weaknesses of some of us "spiritual giants" who come at you via the printed page, the elevated pulpit, or the electronic church—often presenting a push-button gospel which guarantees instant success but seems to work only for those skilled in twisting God's arm or for others more worthy than you to receive heavenly blessings because they have chalked up more Brownie points for good behavior: perfect faith, unparalleled patience, abject humility, pontifical piety, complete forgiveness, helping old ladies across the avenue. . . .

If reading about our feet of clay disturbs you, come back later. But on second thought, if you knew about our hurts and miseries, you could pray for us, couldn't you? Maybe you'd better hang around after all.

Would it shock you to learn that some of us up-front pulpiteers suffer from such highly unheavenly realities as arthritis, gross obesity, ulcers, deadbeat debtors, eyeball imperfections (carefully camouflaged by torturous contact lenses, of course), rear-end collisions, and shiny skinheads festooned more or less attractively with shaggy head doilies?

Would you think less of us—would it clobber your

faith—if you knew that some of us have fractured marriages, carefully hidden for fear of blowing our religious image and losing our badge of respectability and authority in the Christian community?

What if you were to discover that underneath our profusion of hallelujahs with an occasional "Praise the Lord!" were hiding some of the same burdens you bear, resulting in heartache, grief, loneliness, and despair? Things which if openly confessed in some less honest circles would brand us as weak-in-faith, low-grade King's kids at best?

And even while denying the existence of these forbidden weaknesses and failures in *our* lives have some of us riddled you with such accusing Bible bullets as "What you say is what you get!" and "According to your faith be it unto you!" and "By his stripes, you *are* healed!" when your only sin was to ask for prayer for a backache?

Are you a little weary of all that condemnation, and of the easy answers that don't work that some of us Bible-babblers have tossed at you while carefully avoiding such painful questions as "When will my healing be manifested so I can feel it?" and "Why did God heal the servant of the Roman centurion, raise Lazarus from the dead, but refuse to do anything about my own loved one?"

Have you ever dared to question our carefully doctrined "here's the *only* way to do it" theologies (that never worked for you) when you realized that one leper was healed through the dunking method, while ten others received the equally efficacious "go and show" treatment? Or pondered why Jesus healed one blind man with mud, another without mud, and a third on the installment plan?

Maybe you will be glad to know that this book honestly faces these and other sticky real questions arising in the lives of King's kids on Planet Earth, questions which we have mostly ignored in the past or around which we have pussyfooted because the answers didn't fit our simplistic cause-and-effect foolosophies that failed to take into consideration God's design. For some things, there are simply no easy answers, regardless of what some of us Bible-babblers have insisted to the contrary. (Isn't that a relief?) Things like why God said no three times to Paul's request for deliverance, then granted the request of a pagan woman on her very first encounter with Jesus . . . why the great Saint Paul left Trophimus sick at Miletus . . . or why he prescribed booze instead of prayer for his ailing "son" Timothy.

It is my prayer that, in these pages, you will find freedom from the guilt trips laid on you by the insensitive Bible-babblers among us as you learn that we, too, get sick, have divorces in our families, and experience prayer failures just about as often as you do, although heretofore we have kept such grim facts carefully hidden.

It is also my prayer that you will be relieved to learn that your lack of prosperity or good health is not necessarily because of sin on your part, or a negative confession, or a weak faith, but because God is working out a bigger, better plan than any of us have ever suspected or dreamed, a plan not bound to the limits of earth and time, but a plan large enough for eternity.

I pray that you will benefit, as I have, from this often painful attempt at self-honesty, telling it like it is, revealing the other side of the "whole truth," so that if anywhere along the way, at any time in the past, I have caused you to feel like a failure as a King's kid, you may find forgiveness—for yourself and for me. I pray, too, that you may be comforted by the truth that, whatever has happened, "It is God which worketh in you both to will and to do of his good pleasure" (Philippians 2:13).

Join me now in a hallelujah that God's in charge here, and that we are all still unfinished products, King's kids under construction. And do drop me a line to let me know how all things work out for good for you, as together we learn how to let God *be* God—in our lives as well as in the lives of one another.

Harold E. Hill
P.O. Box 8655
Baltimore, MD 21240

2

Confessions of a Former Pharisee

How to Live Like a King's Kid, How to Be a Winner, How to Live in High Victory, How to Flip Your Flab—Forever, Instant Answers for King's Kids in Training, How to Live the Bible Like a King's Kid....

The titles of some of my books sound like glory all the way, don't they? Like I was someone who didn't know what failure was; like I could never find a shred of identification with people who hurt; like all my tribulations had turned out so joyfully, I never shed a tear. Like there were no situations in my life where I was still crying, "Help, Lord!" to the tune of brassy silence from heaven or a loud, "No, a thousand times, no!" Like all the promises of God were immediately manifested as yea and amen in my life on Planet Earth the moment I prayed. Like I'd never asked God for anything without an immediate special-delivery answer in my mailbox. Like the only Scriptures worth looking at were those that spoke of such victory, joy, and deliverance in the here and now, who needs heaven? Like if you would only praise God continually, everything would always turn out all right from your point of view. Well, maybe that's what it *looked* like—which proves that appearances are deceiving.

All the victory reports were and are true, but now it's time for a peek at the other side of the coin: For every high victory I've experienced, there have been a hundred dismal de-

feats and horrendous failures. Furthermore, my experience
indicates that failure is just as essential a part of the Christian's training in this life on Planet Earth as the events that
cause a hallelujah chorus to resound to the rafters.

Are you still with me? Pass 'em the smelling salts, somebody. They didn't expect this from me. Frankly, neither did
I. But hold on. Maybe we both need to hear it.

Successes are very good for beginners at King's-kid living,
maybe even essential, since babies tire easily, and you have
to keep holding their attention by rattling the goodies. But
there's another side to all this, too, and we'll never qualify
for maturity in our King's-kid walk if we don't take a serious look at that other side—and deal with it. The stinky,
yucky side that looks like anything *but* success.

Are you ready?

In the past, I assumed I had to have a positively delicious—even hilarious—answer for everything.

When people asked me, in all seriousness, "Brother Hill,
what should I do if I pray for someone and—gulp—instead
of getting better, he—gulp—croaks?" I answered with a
shoulder-to-shoulder high-victory grin—and maybe an ec-
static chortle or two—"Praise the Lord, brother! Why, you
just bury him and pray for the next one! Chances are, twelve
of 'em won't drop dead in a row. Chuckle, chuckle, chuckle.
The law of averages guarantees that somebody's bound to
recover sooner or later. Har, har, hallelujah!" Sort of eva-
sive, wasn't it?

But when the one who died was their own kid—or a best
friend—my answer was worse than useless. It might even
have made things worse.

Maybe what I should have done was to sit down and cry
with them instead. My friend Allen did that once. His
buddy's teenage daughter had graduated to glory in a freak
accident, and when Allen went to see the daddy, he didn't

boom a hearty, "Praise the Lord, brother! It's all going to work out for good in the fullness of time!" No, Allen didn't say anything. He just grabbed his brother in a gigantic bear hug and then sat down beside him and wept. I understand that no one who went to see the bereaved father helped him more than that man did. No guilt trip, no suggestions of fault placing, just honest grief.

Kind of reminds you of Jesus outside Lazarus' tomb doesn't it.

In the past, things like that—things I knew were real and true—just didn't fit into my theology or doctrine, though, of course, I pretended not to have one, and criticized those who did. Anything that didn't fit my doctrine, I ignored and tried not to think about. But ignoring some things doesn't make them go away. Instead, they keep on getting bigger and bigger, like a leak in the plumbing or a glob of peanut butter on the roof of your mouth. Eventually, such things have to be handled.

In my last book (*How to Live the Bible Like a King's Kid*) I told readers, condescendingly, looking down my shiny nose, that they had my permission to examine the "what ifs" and "yes, buts" of unanswered prayer, of life's tragedies and failures, for themselves if they wanted to do it. But I opted not to join them, thank you.

Don't look now, but I was still dedicated to preserving my image, keeping my eyes squinched shut and my head buried in the sand, pretending the King's-kid walk was always pure glory all the way. Down deep, I knew better—and so did you.

Recent events in my own life have brought me to the point where I'm finally ready to look at failure with you, beginning where it hurts most—with confession of some highly *un*victorious things in my own life as a King's kid. Afterward, if you're still with me, we'll see what, if anything, the Manufacturer's Handbook—that's the Holy Bible—tells us we can do to make things different so God can get some glory out of this mess.

Am *I* ready? Help, Lord!

Let's begin anyway, acknowledging with all we say—and don't say—that God's in charge here, and that He has a purpose for everything that happens in the lives of King's kids on Planet Earth, just as He does in heaven.

"Even the *bad* things?" I hear someone chirping.

Oh, yes! *Especially* the bad things. Jesus came to redeem the bad things, remember? He came because people were sick and sinful, alienated from God, hurting. . . . If we'd all been good as gold, our lives a bowl of cherries, with no problems, He could have stayed in heaven. If we hadn't been all fouled up, we wouldn't have needed a Savior.

"But surely you don't mean that God *sends* the *bad* things, just so He can save us from them?"

Surely I don't. Where the baddies come from is a question I won't pretend to answer in these pages. In the first place, I'm not qualified to judge what is good and what is bad. Ever since Eve succumbed to the forbidden fruit, man has known good and evil but hasn't been able to tell the difference. It happened right there in Eden to Adam and Eve. God said the fruit of the tree of the knowledge of good and evil was bad—it would kill them. Eve thought it looked good and ate it anyway. So much for our ability to know what is bad and what is good.

In the second place, whether God sends the things that look bad, whether He only permits them, or whether He merely uses them once they get here, is beside the point. The fact is, things we judge to be "bad" *are* here, wherever they came from. What we do with them is what matters.

Jesus didn't make any doctrines out of the origin of bad things, and neither will I. No doctrines this trip, only honest reporting of events and a look at some of the principles stated in the Manufacturer's Handbook. All aboard! Let's go.

But first, here's an interesting question for you: Who made the tree of the knowledge of good and evil? I'd never thought about that before, had you? Chew on it while we travel.

PRINCIPLE: "Jesus wept" (John 11:35).

3

Autobiography of an Up-and-Outer

I was born a long time ago—on December 10, 1905, to be exact—to Arthur and Luella (Manley) Hill, way up in Manchester, New Hampshire. I don't happen to remember anything about the day, but I suppose in that geographical territory it had to be cold enough to freeze the proverbial whiskers off a brass monkey—if he had any.

While I was growing up, Daddy was a semi-invalid, and in the terminology of that day, we were poor folks. Today, they'd add a few syllables to the nomenclature and call us "underprivileged" or "disadvantaged," as if the bigger words could take away the sting. But I like the simple truth better, don't you? Maybe the fancy embroidery on the words was invented to go with food stamps, but in that day, there was no such thing as food stamps. Only the poorhouse awaited those who didn't work.

One thing I recall about my childhood is that my clothes were always hand-me-downs. In those days, there was no "one size fits all." Instead, hand-me-downs came in two sizes: too large and too small. I don't know which was worse, to have to use a hank of clothesline rope to gather in the folds of my britches, or to let out the waistline. Both probably helped me learn early to make adjustments for circumstances, whether I liked them or not.

Naturally, I was interested in having something better

than roped-on britches, so by the age of ten, when I read a book about electrical engineering, I decided I would be an engineer when I grew up. Furthermore, I would be so successful, I would earn at least a hundred dollars a week—a king's ransom in those days. And I would be chief engineer of my company. It goes without saying that all my clothes would be tailor-made to fit without clotheslines.

When I told my daddy about my ambition, he nodded wisely and assured me I could have anything I set my heart on if I was willing to work hard enough. I believed him and went about making my fortune in a hurry.

Along the way, several interesting and significant things happened.

When I was fourteen years old, a nice neighbor offered me a cool drink of elderberry wine on a hot day, unintentionally setting in motion a series of events apparently essential in bringing me to where I am today. He didn't know my body chemistry already had me programmed to be an alcoholic, and I didn't know it either. All I know is that from that day on, "demon rum" had an increasingly irresistible attraction for me.

Dad had already warned me that anything alcoholic was "hell juice," to be avoided at all costs. Mother, who was a Christian, told me God would be better pleased with me if I never drank alcohol at all. And the straw that cracked the camel's clavicle was added when Uncle Sam decreed that all alcoholic beverages were off limits to law-abiding Americans.

Then, as in the Garden of Eden, no-nos were automatically guaranteed to create a yes-yes compulsion in the educated idiot box—that's your think tank—of any once-born human being, and so I was headed down Alcohol Road from an early age.

At first, my love affair with the bottle didn't interfere with my other plans. I was still intending to be an engineer—in a hurry. I graduated from high school while I was still wet behind the ears, and had my engineering degree from Pratt Institute by the time I turned twenty-one. I wasn't that much smarter than anybody else—I was just following my daddy's advice and working extra hard.

I was in a hurry to put as much distance as possible between me and those too loose, too tight, never just right, clothesline contraptions. Had I come along forty years later, they might have been the "in" thing, my badge of belonging to some yippee crowd, but as it was, the marks of honest poverty were a shame and a disgrace, to be shed with something approaching the speed of sound.

Five years after graduation, I was chief engineer and vice-president of U.S. operations for a British engineering firm. Seven years later, I was invited to join the parent company in England, from which base I traveled first class as understudy of my British nobleman boss, who was grooming me to represent him worldwide.

Pretty big stuff for a poor country boy, wouldn't you say? Fortunately—or unfortunately—my suits, which were made by London's best tailors, effectively camouflaged a mysterious inner inadequacy and emptiness that grew bigger with every passing year and each important achievement.

A dedicated workaholic (how else could I ever achieve the higher and ever-higher goals I set for myself?), I wound up working away from home for as many as eleven months out of twelve. Needless to say, that was less than the best for the wife and child I left behind while I was building a personal reputation that far exceeded my loftiest childhood dreams. The goal of a hundred bucks a week was left in the dust. It wouldn't have paid my income tax.

If anyone had asked me in those days, I'd have told him that *of course* I loved my little daughter very much. I'd have

been highly indignant had anyone hinted that I was letting
her grow up hardly knowing what a real daddy was. After
all, wasn't I beating my brains out to build security for her
and her mother—security that was spelled out in typical
workaholic fashion in terms of a bigger home, a larger airplane, faster automobiles, and bigger bank accounts?

Patting myself on the back for all my exalted achieve-
ments, I enrolled in advanced studies for top-management
positions until for all practical purposes I was married to my
career. Without realizing what was happening, I had vir-
tually divorced my wife and abandoned my child, pretending all the while that my excessive labors were for their
good.

How stupid can you get?

After nineteen years of working my way up to be the top
man on the North American continent for my employers, I
left them and moved to a four-acre estate in Baltimore
County and into the presidency of my very own brand-new
company. In the eyes of the world, I couldn't have been
more successful. And of course, the responsibility for my
own business meant I had perfect, unarguable reasons for
working harder than ever—seven days a week, from dawn
till dark—keeping everything running smoothly. It was still
all for the wife and kid, you understand, although admittedly I might not have recognized them if we had bumped
into one another on the sidewalk in broad daylight.

On the outside, things continued to look pretty good, but
inside, there was that baffling vacuum that grew more and
more insatiable. Talk about black holes! There was a dark
emptiness inside me that swooshed everything I fed it into
oblivion faster than a kid with six friends and five pieces of
bubblegum.

In a frantic effort to cope with the growing nothingness, I
added several more slugs of Four Roses to my nightly in-

take. When anyone had the audacious effrontery to mention it, suggesting I should consider "cutting down," I'd cut him down on the spot. Backing away, I'd eyeball him into an abject apology with my ironclad excuse, "You dimwit! In this business, I *have* to drink with my clients! Don't you know *anything?*"

On the rare occasions when that approach failed to wilt the offenders right down to their skivvies, I'd let it be *their* problem. No one was going to tell *me* what to do.

Inevitably, I kept adding more and more alcohol to my life-style until I was almost sloshing in my efforts to fill up the yawning chasm of an emptiness that kept growing larger and larger. The more I fed it, the emptier it got. It didn't make sense. If I could have reached past my epiglottis to measure the vacuum inside me, I'm sure I'd have found it was bigger than I was.

Every time I thought about the depressing aspects of that, I shuddered and upped my intake of booze another notch. Finally, the demon spirits in liquid form had usurped the place of all the comforts of home, which by now were practically nonexistent, thanks to my own colossally counterproductive willpower efforts.

One day, it all caught up with me where it hurts.

My daughter, Linda, then in her teens, suggested I might be drinking too much. "Who, me? I never drink in the daytime," I argued. Then my wife, Ruth, made little noises about leaving me if I continued to overdo it in the imbibing department. But even those warnings of impending disaster didn't wake me up until one night when I saw myself headed for total destruction. You can read all the gruesome details in *How to Live Like a King's Kid.* At any rate, with feelings at zero, even though materially I was hugely successful, I heard these startling words come from my previously self-sufficient lips: "God, help me!"

That was quite a switch from "I can do it myself." It was a prayer of desperation, straight from the heart, with no strings attached. And help me He did, just as He promised He would in Acts 2:21, though I didn't know the Scripture at that time: "And it shall come to pass, that whosoever shall call upon the name of the Lord shall be saved."

I had become a whosoever by calling upon the name of the Lord, and the following week I found myself at a meeting of Alcoholics Anonymous. By God's grace and the help of that organization, I haven't had a single drink in the thirty years that have passed since that day. In AA, they assured me that I need not be a down-and-outer to receive instant cutoff from alcohol. And they also told me, "If you stay with us and are *not* an alcoholic, you'll never become one. Furthermore, if you *are* one, you'll never get any worse."

Wisdom from above! Praise God!

PRINCIPLE: "I denied myself nothing my eyes desired; I refused my heart no pleasure. My heart took delight in all my work, and this was the reward for all my labor. Yet when I surveyed all that my hands had done and what I had toiled to achieve, everything was meaningless, a chasing after the wind; nothing was gained under the sun" (Ecclesiastes 2:10, 11 NIV).

4

A Few Questions

Now here's as good a place as any to stop and look back at my initial, long-ago failures and ask a few questions.

For openers, think about all the folks who must have prayed for me during all those years when I was drinking more and more and enjoying life less and less. Where was God?

Do you suppose He was listening to the supplications of the saints who were wearing out their kneecaps praying that I would straighten up and fly right? Do you suppose He heard their intercessions when they fasted and prayed and begged God to keep me from taking that next drink—even while I was belting it down and ordering another double? Do you suppose He was paying any attention when my wife was sitting with a decorous Episcopal doily on her head, beseeching heaven to get me to stop doing all the bad things I was into and to settle down and be a good husband and father?

It was surely God's will for me to behave myself—wasn't it?

Where *was* God when I was waxing worse and worse? Out to lunch? Taking a nap? Or was He busy cooking up an "abundantly, above all that we ask or think" answer to the prayers for me?

Let's look for a minute at all those things in the light of my ministry today.

What would have happened, for instance, if those prayers "for my own good" had been answered before God's fullness of time? If I had stopped drinking through some kind of reliance on my own willpower? If I had used my common sense and altered my life-style sufficiently that I and other people could have stood it?

What would have happened?

Nobody can say for sure, but it just might be that I would have been cheated out of the greatest opportunity for fulfillment a man can ever have—getting to know the King of the Universe on a first-name basis and having the privilege of sharing Him with others.

Since alcohol was the only thing in my life I hadn't been able to handle, the only thing that could make me cry out, "God, help me!" could it actually have been *good*, maybe, in God's way of looking at things, that I had turned out to be an alcoholic, someone who couldn't stay sober without Him? Given all the circumstances—especially God's plan for my life—could my being an alcoholic have been a deliberate part of God's plan for me?

Don't leave now; think about it some more. Could those years that were so full of agony for me and my family have been an essential part of the tailor-made preparation and training I needed in order to fulfill God's purpose when He chose me, as He says in 1 Peter 2:9? "... to proclaim the wonderful acts of God ..." (TEV).

Before you dismiss the whole idea as being heretical in terms of man-made doctrines of your church or your favorite evangelist who insists that God does only "good things"—by his and our own definition of "good," of course—look with me at a couple of cases in the pages of the Manufacturer's Handbook.

We'd have missed a lot, wouldn't we, if Daniel had prayed to be kept out of the lions' den and God had answered his prayer, just like that. I mean, it made a whole lot more exciting adventure to be thrown into the den and kept out of the lions' mouths, didn't it? And think of the faith builder we'd been cheated of if Meshach, Shadrach, and Abednego hadn't had a chance to prove God was in charge in the midst of a fiery furnace.

From our vantage point, it was good that those things happened, wasn't it, though at the time they must have looked like the pits.

Some days, I can look around me and see so much good coming out of "bad" things, I couldn't believe it possible if I didn't know Jesus.

Are there some things in our lives for which we give Satan the credit when all the time it is God working in us to will and to do of *His* good pleasure (Philippians 2:13) if folks will just trust Him?

Wait a minute. I seem to hear somebody squawking that the "Lions' Club luncheon" and "Nebuchadnezzar's barbecue pit" were Old Testament events that don't have anything to do with today. Let's turn to the New Testament, then, and pick up echoes of the dialogue Jesus had one day with the disciples who were questioning Him about the man who was born blind (John 9).

"Why was this man born blind?" they asked Him. And before he could open His mouth to answer, they had indicated the direction their own answers would have taken, based on their erroneous theology that said what they called imperfection was generally someone's fault. They offered Him a multiple-choice question—a presumptuous sin if I've ever heard one:

"Did he sin, or was it his parents' sin that caused him to be born blind?" they wanted to know, confident Jesus' answer would blame somebody.

"None of the above," He said. (I'm paraphrasing, of course.) He went on to buffalo them completely and horse up all their careful, well-meaning doctrines of condemnation when He replied, "It wasn't his sin—or the sin of his parents—that caused him to be born blind. His blindness was for the purpose of showing God's power in healing him."

Wow! Get a load of that! What a doctrine blaster! In other words, God was in charge all along—from before the foundation of the world, maybe? (Ephesians 1:4)—and He had a specific purpose for blindness in that man's life. Blindness was apparently an essential part of God's plan until the fullness of time came along and Jesus healed him. If he had been healed ahead of time—or hadn't been blind at all—he could have spoiled the whole program.

Could it be that my alcoholism manifested itself so that God would be able to show His power when I turned to Him for help, and then I would be equipped to go brag about God and what He had done for me? An "after" picture of a man doesn't say much without a "before" picture alongside it, does it?

Now don't leap to conclusions the way Paul's hearers did one day when he was explaining some similar things to them. Don't decide, "Well, if there's more grace where there's more sin, shouldn't we sin up a storm so God will get more glory?"

That question is just as silly as it sounds to your ears, and I'd have to answer it the same way Paul did: "Drop dead!" He meant dead to sin, of course, and added, "From now on, live for God." (Turn to Romans 6 if you want to get the full flavor of all Paul had to say about it.)

It's all right to speculate about some of these things if you can trust yourself to do it without locking yourself into a theology about them. Could it be, for instance, that the particular, unique catastrophe of your life—whatever it is— came along so that God could get your attention and then be glorified when His power came along to deliver you?

And maybe "the sooner the better" is a concept that doesn't always fit in with God's fullness-of-time intentions. Do you remember what He said about timing? It's so good, I want to quote it all, just as He put it in the mouth—or pen—of His servant Peter:

> But there is one thing, my friends, that you must never forget: that with the Lord, "a day" can mean a thousand years, and a thousand years is like a day. The Lord is not being slow to carry out his promises, as anybody else might be called slow; but he is being patient with you all, wanting nobody to be lost and everybody to be brought to change his ways.
>
> 2 Peter 3:8, 9 JERUSALEM

I'm thankful He was patient with me, aren't you?

If a man was into the doctrinal-theology manufacturing business, he could almost take that Peter talk and whomp up a theology that said nobody would ever get healed of alcoholism—or anything else—until it got bad enough that the person would be so desperate he'd gladly accept salvation as part of the package. But it's good we're not in the theology-making business, because it doesn't work out that way every time. We're letting God be God for a change!

I have seen cases where God moved so fast in someone's life that interested bystanders said, "Boy! He was lucky he didn't break his leg!" and robbed God of all the glory for mending a broken leg in the twinkling of an eye.

And if He moved a little more slowly than that, but faster than the medical charts say is possible, to heal what had all the signs of a terminal disease, scoffers settled it with a nonchalant, "Oh. Wrong diagnosis, huh?" and God was robbed again.

Let's look at another New Testament example before we move on.

One day Jesus was going about His business when a messenger came and told Him His friend Lazarus was sick (John 11). Did Jesus say the word and heal him from a distance as He had done in the case of the centurion's servant?

No. He didn't even try to do that, but said, ". . . this has happened in order to bring glory to God, and it will be the means by which the Son of God will receive glory" (John 11:4 TEV).

Has your favorite faith teacher ever hinted that sickness could *ever* be used to glorify God? I've heard some say it *couldn't*, but in this case Jesus seemed to be on the other side of the fence.

He didn't even hurry to go to Lazarus, but deliberately stayed two days longer where He was, only two miles away. It was only after He knew Lazarus was dead that He agreed to go to him! Talk about backward! Which one of us would have been that negligent? And finally, Jesus even said, "Lazarus is dead, and for your sake I am *glad* I was not there, *so that you may believe . . .*" (John 11:14 NIV, my italics). We seem to have run into a special purpose again. What was His purpose this time? Apparently He wanted the people to believe He could raise a man from the dead when he'd been in the tomb four days. That was a new idea!

The people already knew He could cure blindness that had lasted a long time; now He wanted them to know He could cure deadness, too, and He needed a corpse to prove it.

Lazarus must have been willing to be the corpse. He came

forth, and many people *believed* as a result of what happened that day. Getting people to *believe* must have had a high priority in Jesus' earthly ministry. So maybe we need some of the same?

Could that be one reason God does some of the things He does today—not to keep us comfortable in this life, but to get us in a position where we are sufficiently *un*comfortable that we will turn to Him and *believe* He can make a difference?

As a bottom line for this chapter, then, could we agree that when God's in charge of our lives, anything can happen? We can't legislate any rigid doctrines about anything, because we just don't know what *all* His purposes are or how He plans to use each unique individual to accomplish them. Take Judas, for example, ". . . the one doomed to destruction so that Scripture would be fulfilled" (John 17:12 NIV).

We can't even say whether something is good or bad with any degree of accuracy, because we don't look at things the way God does, not even in the same time frame, since a thousand years are like a day to Him. We aren't equipped to see the end from the beginning. He is. Hallelujah!

The day I had my first drink and the day I had my last one were separated by many years of misery for me and many others, before I learned to look at things as God sees them, through the mind of Christ instead of being influenced by the external symptoms of my disease. But in God's sight, it all happened in the single twinkling of an eye. He was working in eternity to turn the whole gloppy mess into glory.

Don't look now, but that crud you heard thudding to the floor at your feet just might have been some dead theology. Feel free to leave it there, and let's move on. Don't bother to resurrect the mess. The more dead theology we can get rid of this trip, the better off we'll be.

PRINCIPLE: "For my thoughts are not your thoughts, neither are your ways my ways, saith the Lord. For as the heavens are higher than the earth, so are my ways higher than your ways, and my thoughts than your thoughts" (Isaiah 55:8, 9).

5

Different as Two Snowflakes

Did my life turn into a happily-ever-after romance full of only upbeat adventures once I had hollered to the Lord for help and He had used Alcoholics Anonymous to put a stopper on my drinking? Only temporarily. Then disaster *really* set in!

Contrary to the best Alcoholics Anonymous principles, I actually accentuated my workaholic life-style that kept me away from home, giving me further "justifiable" excuses for not being the husband and father I should have been. Instead of spending some of my sober hours with the wife and child as suggested by AA, I got into the "help others" program of AA—twenty-four hours a day. As far as family ties were concerned, they slowly but surely came totally unraveled through my complete neglect of all family responsibilities, except for providing in a material way for needs that could be met with the contents of a bulging bank account and a checkbook. That combination has to be the world's most pitiful substitute for loving concern.

"I almost wish you were back into drinking again," my wife, Ruth, sighed one night as I prepared to leave home for what could well turn into another all-night vigil with a sick alcoholic.

"You've got to be kidding!" I sputtered in self-righteous indignation. (I've never heard of any other kind, have you?)

l was stopped dead in my tracks, remembering how I used to stagger home in the wee hours, barely coherent, knocking over furniture as I lurched through the living room trying to land on the couch. She thought *that* was better than *this?*

"No, I'm perfectly serious," she insisted. "Back when you were drinking, I used to know where you were once in a while. I could see you, even if you were a little blurry. But now I never see you at all except occasionally at mealtimes, and then you're usually late."

How could I defend myself? It was all too true—and totally unacceptable to my pride and ego. So I refused to do anything about it. Worse, I wouldn't even *acknowledge* it, and the canyon between us yawned a little wider as I continued on my workaholic way, ego-tripping my "but Joe *needs* me!" rationalization into the death throes of a marriage being held together only to maintain a home for our daughter and to put up a good front of respectability for the community. Hardly a sound basis for loving fulfillment of a "till death us do part" kind of contract. Clothesline rope might have worked better.

Actually, death had already parted us. That we were still walking around at the same address and wearing the same last name didn't alter the fact that our so-called marriage was already deader than a doornail.

The stage was set—and I had inadvertently, unconsciously, but oh, so expertly, done it myself. Then the inevitable happened. You guessed it. In walked Mr. Wonderful, practically by my invitation. He was a real Prince Charming, teeth and all, and he swooped up my bride and carried her off. With that, what pitiful remnants were left of a twenty-five-year-old marriage completely disintegrated.

Though everyone else had seen the signs and tried to tell me, it took me completely by surprise when my carefully assembled empire blew up in my face. Alcoholism, well

named a family disease, coupled with my workaholic, per-
fectionist life-style, had scuttled family relationships and all
affection. "Success" had done its job well. My marriage was
smashed.

When the initial shock suffered by my pride and ego had
worn off, sudden rage and anger took over, and I set out to
avenge my loss of that all-important self-image which had to
be preserved at all costs, even the cost of a human life.

"They can't do that to me! I'll fix them!" became my every
waking thought. I was rarely without a loaded gun in my
pocket, so as to be ready for the kill when the quarry came
into range. But when I stalked Romeo into my sights one
night, to my utter frustration, I couldn't pull the trigger. It
wasn't that I changed my mind—my hand just wouldn't
work. My trigger finger refused to budge, and the culprit
split the scene, his skin intact.

Even *I* was bright enough to recognize that had to be God
in operation in an awesome, totally unexpected kind of reality. Did it happen because in AA I had completed the third
step of the program by making a decision to turn my life and
will over to the care of God as I understood Him? I didn't
know, but I was ready for some answers.

That's the night I went to the home of my friend Ed and
met Jesus. (Again, you can read all the details in *How to
Live Like a King's Kid.*) From that night on, all the thirst for
murderous revenge was gone, and in its place was a great
cleansing flood of peace and joy.

God had taken all the ingredients for a tragedy and used
them to get my attention. "Satan meant it for evil, but God
used it for good," Joseph of the coat of many colors would
have said.

God seems to do that often in the case of rebellious people, doesn't He. I mean, haven't you heard of literally hun-

dreds of folks who had no use for God until something terrible happened in their lives? The bookstore shelves are filled with their testimonies. Could God possibly be in charge of things like that?

Sure, I know as well as you do that some folks surrender to God when they're cold sober, not mad at anybody, and have just come to the end of a calm and peaceful day, but some of us refuse to come that easily. God has to find a way to let us get into a position to receive heaven's best. That can't happen when our self-made empires stand in the way, so something has to crumble. In my case, a fractured marriage became the matrix for a far greater and more essential union—between Jesus the Bridegroom and myself, a member of the Body of Christ.

I can hear you saying, "Brother Hill, do you mean to stand there and tell me that God puts people into circumstances as raunchy as all that just to get them saved?"

Whoa, there! I didn't say anything of the kind. I'm not making generalizations or inventing doctrines or theologies on this trip, remember? Don't you do it either. I'm simply reporting, honestly, what has happened in my case. Maybe God takes us by the easiest route we'll agree to come. I was a tough customer, that's all—about like old Pharaoh—making it hard for everybody concerned. I'm not advocating that anybody be an alcoholic, a workaholic, neglect his wife and kid so terribly that the marriage blows to smithereens and all hell breaks loose, just so the poor slob can get saved. I hope you can come by an easier route than that.

The evidence, as I look around me, is that nobody has to come by the same route that anyone else has taken. People seem to be like snowflakes or thumbprints: no two alike. Similar sometimes, but never identical. If you were able to come to God by looking up into some fleecy white clouds on a bright summer day while you were doing nothing more traumatic than walking to school, or hanging clothes on the line, or picking up the evening paper from the no-weeds grass of your front lawn, more power to you. I wish we could all enter the kingdom as happily as that. But the facts indicate that some of us are too hardheaded.

When you come right down to it, God must find it very difficult to bless people like me, because our hands are usually so full of filthy rags—the products of our own best self-efforts—we can't hold anything else, no matter how good it is. I'm just glad He found a way to empty my hands so He could move into my life. Whatever it cost, it had to be the biggest bargain in the basement when I traded my own down-the-tube failure for the wonders of eternal life.

But the Good News is that you don't have to wait for hell to take over before you change your direction to heaven. Could it be that because I've gone through it the hard way, you can learn something vicariously and come by an easy route? I hope so. If you're ready to do it now, there's no waiting list. Just try this prayer on for size:

> Lord Jesus, thank You for loving me enough to get my attention today, however You had to do it. I confess that I'm a sinner, that You are the risen-from-the-dead Son of the Almighty God, and I invite You to come into my heart and take over my life and forgive all my sins. In the perfect name of Jesus. Amen.

If you said it and really meant it, you're in. Welcome to the life of a King's kid. Now that I'm honest, reporting the whole truth, I can't promise you that it will all be easy or fun. But I can promise that God's in charge of it all, and that after this life is over, you won't be down the tube with dirty old sinners, but will spend the rest of eternity in Gloryland with Jesus.

That will be good—all the way—by *anybody's* definition.

PRINCIPLE: "From one man he created all races of mankind and made them live throughout the whole earth. He himself fixed beforehand the exact times and the limits of the places where they would live. He did this so that they would look for him, and perhaps find him as they felt around for him" (Acts 17:26, 27 TEV).

6

Till Death Us Do Part

"Well, but Brother Hill, I thought I heard you say that your wife was back at home answering the telephone."

You probably did. And she probably was. Everywhere I went, for years, when people would ask me about my wife, mostly I'd smile and say she was at home answering the telephone. She still is, as a matter of fact. Our phone rings a lot. But we decided back in the first chapter of this book that appearances were deceiving, didn't we? Let me explain.

After I met Jesus, my life began to have real meaning and purpose for the first time. I was able to deliver the Good News about a personal God not only to my immediate circle of friends, but increasingly to a wider world. God opened doors to Europe and the United States, to the up-and-outers as well as to the down-and-outers—those from Yale as well as from jail—all of whom are gutter bums without Jesus, the only difference being the height of a curbstone, as I like to say. I've been able to give my witness to my former top-management buddies, some of whom, like the jet set and royalty of Europe with whom I traveled in years past, have been my willing listeners when I tell them the Good News.

"You don't have to drink or drug yourself to death or jump out of windows," I can tell them. "There's a better way to handle this life. Let me tell you what I've found." Some of them listen, and some of them get saved, and that makes it all worth the price which once seemed too great for my ego and pride to bear.

But in the midst of all that glory, my marital status is still best described as nonexistent. The woman called my wife does answer the telephone and keep house. I write the checks. That's been the extent of our "wedded bliss" for the last twenty-seven years, ever since Mr. Wonderful sent her back home and I opened the door and let her in.

Prayer? Yes, there have been thousands of prayers over dozens of years, begging Jesus to really bring Hal and Ruth back together as man and wife, but for some reason, known only to God, it hasn't happened. Yes, we still live in the same house. Yes, we have consulted the best Christian counselors and psychiatrists. You name it: if it's any kind of remedy recommended for broken marriages, we've tried it. But we continue to coexist in a marriage that's a marriage in name only. I'm not proud of it. I'm just reporting how it is with me. Total failure.

Have I asked God, "Why me, Lord?" Sure. A thousand times, at least. But for years I didn't hear any answer. Still, I knew He was in charge here—of happy situations and hurting ones—and I knew He was working it for good for those who loved Him, those who were called according to His purpose, including me (Romans 8:28).

What on earth *is* Your purpose in this, Lord?

I still don't know the whole answer, but you might be interested in some of the ways I've seen Him use—for good—my failure in this area of my life. He's shown me repeatedly over the last quarter of a century of ministry that He can use anything for His glory that's really turned over to Him.

How does God use a broken marriage? For one thing, in my own case, lately—ever since I decided to come out in the

open and be honest about it—He's been using my circumstances to give me compassion and understanding for others
in the same boat. That's been important, because often
"good church folks" have nothing to offer divorced people
other than a self-righteous attitude of rejection. I had that
kind of attitude for years, even after the breakup of my own
marriage, while I was still pretending it was lovey-dovey because I thought that would please the brethren.

You remember what Paul said about pleasing men, don't
you? "... am I trying to please men?" he asked. "If I were
still trying to please men, I would not be a servant of Christ"
(Galatians 1:10 NIV). Pleasing men is not something God
recommends. I'm sorry, Lord. I won't do it again.

I nearly destroyed my own daughter when she was on the
verge of divorce and I counseled her, in no uncertain terms,
"Baby, you married him. He's yours. You're stuck with him
for all eternity."

Once God opened my eyes, insisting I drag my ostrich
head out of the sand and be honest, I had to admit I had
treated Linda very unreasonably. I thank God I've been
able to confess my religious snobbery, based on adherence
to a church doctrine that made me pretend I had a beauti-
fully intact marriage when it was actually more like a sepul-
cher, full of dead men's bones.

Linda is divorced now and remarried to a fine, loving
man. But my legalistically ministered doctrines nearly killed
her. I literally drove her out of Christian fellowship for
longer than I care to remember.

Have you noticed lately, as I have, that many leading
ministers, some of whom have been hard on divorced people, have been having to experience that trauma in their own
immediate families? I could name a whole handful of the
biggies from coast to coast who have been put in a position

of learning through personal experience about the whole divorce-and-remarriage syndrome. Before it happened, perhaps they were like me—in bondage to doctrines based on the letter of the law that kills. Now together we can examine the whole matter in the light of love—the most excellent way of all.

When Jesus said, "Love the Lord your God with all your heart, with all your soul, and with all your mind," and "Love your neighbor as you love yourself," and added, "The whole Law of Moses and the teachings of the prophets depend on these two commandments" (Matthew 22:37–40 TEV), He wasn't saying we were to shun people who had made a marriage mistake and consign them to the pit. But we've certainly acted like it in many of our churches. To some of us, it was such a valuable self-justification weapon to rationalize our errors!

In considering other Scriptures that could apply, I remember the disciples came to Jesus and asked Him, "What is the work God wants us to do?" (*see* John 6:28).

He didn't say, "Stay married to the wife of your youth or you'll go straight to hell." He said, "This is the work God wants you to do: believe in the one he sent" (John 6:29 TEV). When we *believe* in Him according to the meaning of the Greek word as it is explained in the Amplified Bible, we do far more than give mental assent to a proposition. Literally, to *believe* is "to adhere to, cleave to; to trust, to have faith in; to rely on." Then, as the Amplified version puts it, to " 'believe on the Lord Jesus Christ . . . ' really means *to have an absolute personal reliance upon the Lord Jesus Christ as Saviour*" (Publisher's Foreword). And when you're believing on Him in that way, you're not governing your life—or attempting to govern anyone else's life—by adherence to a rigid set of rules. Instead, you're looking to Him for guidance in every unique situation, and counseling others, not by rules but by something far higher than rules—by the way of love.

Now let's look at it from a slightly different angle for a minute.

There is a principle in life, the mirror principle, which says that whatever you criticize in others is exactly what you may expect to happen to you. That's just one of the many ways of expressing the truth of Romans 2:1 (PHILLIPS), which says :

> Now if you feel inclined to set yourself up as a judge of those who sin, let me assure you, whoever you are, that you are in no position to do so. For at whatever point you condemn others you automatically condemn yourself, since you, the judge, commit the same sins.

Pretty strong stuff, isn't it! And I saw it in action. And repented. The critical attitude toward divorced folks which was my badge of respectability for so many years has been replaced with a heart that identifies with their hurts and griefs. Once, I pointed to the sinners and said, "Well, at least I'm not *that* bad." Now I sit with them and say, "I know how you feel."

Divorce happens to be a fact of life with multitudes these days. No one is immune. What are you going to do—judge them or comfort them? And who can comfort them and minister to them except someone whom God has equipped to understand how terribly they hurt? It's a fellowship of suffering.

When the Manufacturer's Handbook says of Jesus, "Though he were a Son, yet learned he obedience by the things which he suffered" (Hebrews 5:8), I find myself asking, "If the Son of God had to suffer, why *not* us?"

As if to say, "Right on!" Paul said he yearned to know "the fellowship of His sufferings" (Philippians 3:10). All that *has* to mean something.

I'm so thankful that God's standards are far greater than ours, and that our self-made "holiness measurements" of one another mean little or nothing to Him. Which one of us, for instance, would have supposed God could still make use of David after he had committed adultery with Bathsheba and arranged for her husband Uriah to be killed? And yet God called this adulterer, this murderer, a man after His own heart (Acts 13:22). Which one of us would have picked the prostitute Rahab for a special assignment in the kingdom, or would have let someone out of whom we had cast seven devils wash *our* feet?

I'm so glad we serve a forgiving God, aren't you? And He tells us to forgive one another as He forgives us. That ought to be real liberation.

Do I hear a glory shout?

The statement in the Manufacturer's Handbook, "He giveth and He taketh away" (*see* Job 1:21), *could* apply to loved ones, valued possessions, and yes, even marriages which, while of great value in the scheme of things in this life, are set aside when God has something different (maybe even better?) for a specific person to equip him for the purpose God has designed him to fulfill.

At this point, someone is seeing red and whispering in a shocked undertone, "Situational ethics—from Hill?" And someone else, not quite so sotto voce, comes forth with, "Why, Brother Hill is condoning—or even advocating—divorce!"

For the record, I'm doing no such thing. We're not making theologies, remember? I'm simply reporting how it stands with me and honestly facing facts as they exist in many of our churches today where divorced folks are often made to feel like second-class citizens in the kingdom of heaven.

Think I'm exaggerating? If you're blessed to be in a church that is *not* like that, maybe you need to know how it is in other places.

Born again and filled with the Spirit, Mary and John were a joy to their local church fellowship, and everyone thought they had it all together. Then came the flabbergasting day when John left town, divorced his wife, and took off with another woman after openly confessing that those were his intentions and daring anybody to do anything about it.

Did everyone flock to Mary to comfort her? Far from it! Suddenly she was a spiritual outcast, unwelcome as a peacock with no plumes, utterly condemned by one of the elders who told her that maybe preparing better meals and darning John's socks with softer thread would have saved the marriage.

What's your opinion?

Does all this blaming business ring any bells for you in connection with Jesus' conversation with the disciples about the blind man? Did the divorce have to be Mary's fault at all—or his? Or was God in charge even here, working out something we have as yet failed to see?

I don't know. I prefer to let God be God!

The coup de grace came as Mary knelt at the altar rail that morning in abject misery. (If you hear of any other kind of misery among divorced folks, let me know.) A retired preacher and member of that highly spiritual fellowship came over to Mary, raised his hands into the air, and shouted—with several octaves of tremolos—for all to hear, "Heavenly Father, have mercy on this poor, fallen woman. Save her, Lord, and show her the error of her wicked ways. For Christ's sake. Amen."

Before being deserted by good old John, she had been "Sister Mary," but now all that had changed. She was absolutely rejected by many of those beautiful folks who simply could not identify with her—because they had not been down that road. Understandably, their attitude was exactly what mine had formerly been, that divorce is worse than the pits and consigns one irrevocably and for all eternity to second-grade status in God's family.

Thank God *He* doesn't see it that way!

Would Jesus have condemned Mary? Not on your life, but her self-righteous *condemners* might have had some problems with Him.

Maybe it has been necessary for some of us former Pharisees to suffer similar agony so we would get off our high horses of condemnation in circumstances of this kind, and be His agents of reconciliation, conformed to His way of thinking—the way of forgiveness and love.

Well, we've stirred up quite a mess of snakes on this subject, haven't we. Can we find a bottom line in all of it? For me, part of it seems to be summed up in the words of 2 Corinthians 1:3–5 NIV:

> Praise be to the God and Father of our Lord Jesus Christ, the Father of compassion and the God of all comfort, who comforts us in all our troubles, so that we can comfort those in any trouble with the comfort we ourselves have received from God. For just as the sufferings of Christ flow over into our lives, so also through Christ our comfort overflows.

As I see it, that's part of what being King's kids is all about, not just hallelujahing about the victories, but also sharing the comforts God has brought to us in our miseries and thereby fulfilling part of our assignment as King's kids in this life: bearing one another's burdens. According to the Sermon on the Mount, it is through comforting others, i.e., being peacemakers, that we come to be called the children of God—King's kids.

God seems to have used my "bad" for "good" in more ways than one. Not only has He set me free from condemning others but He has also used my broken family ties to free me for traveling worldwide and sharing my wonderful Jesus with "whosoever will" instead of settling down in the old rocking chair, which would indeed have held some attraction for one at my "threescore and fifteen" level of life, given an environment of perfect domestic bliss. Since that environment is lacking. . . .

What happened to me is just one more example of how God lets Romans 8:28 come alive when we simply take God at His Word and realize that His ways are often contrary to our best church doctrines. When we let Him be God, in charge of our lives and the lives of others, He can truly work all things together for good—both His and ours.

Meanwhile, do I continue to pray that God will make what looks—and feels—like a second-best situation turn out all right? Of course. Every day of my life. In the meantime, I've found Paul is right when he says that His grace is sufficient. It is.

Now, if you happen to have a marriage that was made in heaven, keep praising God for it. Know that it's His gift to you, for reasons of His own, and not anything you could possibly have earned or merited. If you don't develop a superior attitude about it, you may even be able to keep it.

PRINCIPLE: "For God had said to Moses, 'If I want to be kind to someone, I will. And I will take pity on anyone I want to.' And so God's blessings are not given just because someone decides to have them or works hard to get them. They are given because God takes pity on those he wants to" (Romans 9:15, 16 TLB).

7

For Richer or Poorer— and Poorer

Another area of life's problems in which I have prayed much with unbelievably poor results has been in the area of finances, more specifically in the sticky matter of people who owe me money and refuse to part with it. I'm still praying about three situations in which I loaned large sums of money—representing my entire retirement fund—to folks whose impeccable reputations seemed to be all the assurance I needed that they would pay it back, according to the terms on which we mutually agreed.

They didn't.

I prayed.

They still didn't.

I prayed again—and registered just about 100 percent failure on all my prayers. Year after year I waited in vain for God to move them to pay me back, even *without* interest, at least *part* of what I loaned them. Results? A big, fat blank. The answer continued to be a silent no from the Lord and an even greater negative silence from the brethren using my bucks.

How come? Didn't God *want* me to have the money that I'd put to work for Him?

Just recently the Lord has begun to show me some of the many factors which might be involved in my case—or yours. Care to hear them?

To begin with, *sometimes*—no doctrines, remember—unpaid debts of this nature have a tendency to crop up in the lives of King's kids whose secret security is founded on the rock of the Fat Wallet. In order for that false god to be exposed and deposed, so we won't live in violation of the First Commandment to have no other gods before Him, God strips us down to having to trust him instead of guaranteed income for the bare essentials of everyday living. In that position, we may be better able to recognize our real problem—which may not be tardy debtors at all, but a divided mind about our ultimate security.

When our minds are divided between God on one hand and earthly riches on the other, the double vision interferes with a right relationship with God, who wants to single-handedly supply our every need out of the abundance of His riches in glory through Christ Jesus.

It must be a great handicap for God to try to be in charge here whenever my attitude is ever so slightly divided between Him and some worldly treasure, even when I seem completely justified, as the world looks at it. A King's kid living in high victory bases his attitude on better principles than the normal, logical way of looking at things. After all, "He must increase, but I must decrease" (John 3:30), in terms of my ownership of worldly things, doesn't make too much sense in the human think tank. But He's got a higher calling for us: to have our minds reprogrammed to contain His mind.

(By the way, keeping one eye on God and the other eye on your bank balance can make you kind of cross-eyed, had you ever noticed?)

Instead of answering my constant cry for restitution—with interest—God might have been dealing with my need to be set free from the poverty syndrome inherited from my belted-with-clothesline days. Actually, it went back even further than that, to Granddaddy Adam in the Garden of Eden, whose best effort to provide his own security turned out to be a drafty fig leaf.

Having grown up on the edge of poverty, I confess that I *did* have a burning obsession to have enough money in the bank to take care of all my needs in the foreseeable future. As various successes came my way, naturally I tried to put as many dollars as possible between poverty and me. When I met Jesus and attempted to turn all my dependence for security over to Him, I still had my former attitude toward money, considering it essential to my well-being. To a considerable degree, the Lord had loosened my purse strings, breaking the bondage of the wallet through His system called tithing, but although I was a tither, admittedly my attitude needed further improvement. (See *How to Live Like a King's Kid* for an explanation of how this tithing business works.)

As I understand it, money represents a portion of our very lives, sold to our employer for so many dollars, and is therefore a good foundation checkout as to where our security lies. If it is in people, places, or things—including money— God loves us enough to allow circumstances to set us free from that bondage—even at the expense of my retirement fund. And He will even let Christian brethren be the ones who fleece me!

"The love of money is the root of all evil" (1 Timothy 6:10) is the way God reminds us of these things in the Manufacturer's Handbook. For a long time, I went around misquoting that verse this way: "Money is the root of all evil," which, of course, is not the case.

Because God loves us, He will go to great lengths to see to it that we can never find complete contentment with the things of this world. I've learned that false gods often involve satisfaction with anything having to do with our accomplishments and are often revealed when we talk in terms of *my* money, *my* home, *my* job, *my* children, *my* ministry. . . . That rug can be neatly pulled out from under anybody by Isaiah 26:12, which reminds us of the truth of these things: "Lord . . . all that we have accomplished you have done for us" (NIV). Kind of a mindblower, that verse. The first time I saw it, it cut me down to size.

Reminded that I am only a steward, never an owner, of all things entrusted to my care, including green stuff, I have a license to keep going to the King with sticky money problems which no amount of human manipulation or legal action can solve.

But did learning these things make my financial situation clear up immediately? Did checks of restitution show up in my mailbox with profound apologies for the delay and an overgenerous amount of interest? No way. Still not a cheep out of my debtors.

What else was I supposed to learn, for heaven's sake?

Well, there was a further matter of attitude, He seemed to tell me: my attitude toward the folks who were keeping me broke.

For one thing, I was still blaming myself for trusting such untrustworthy folks: "I should have known they'd scalp me if they thought they could get away with it."

That was like saying, "God's in charge here—except of my wrong decisions, of course," and I had opened myself to bitterness. But when I changed my mind and chose to say, "Praise the Lord! He's even in charge of my bad judgments and wrong decisions," then it became His problem, not mine, and I could claim His promise that He would work it all out for good and glory for Himself and deliverance for all His young 'uns. That it was taking longer for God to work out than I thought would be the case was His business, not mine. I knew God wasn't rushed—eternity has barely begun.

Another insight He's given me into these prayer "failures" is that some of them could be related to a critical spirit, a superior attitude toward the way others handle their problems in these same areas. I might have expressed my perfect image before the church in terms like these:

"I would, of course, *never* resent a brother for owing me money. Christians just never do these things—*do* they?" How could I better learn to get down off my high horse than to be put in a position where it happened to me?

Another Scripture I've found intriguing is 2 Timothy 2:25, 26. Speaking to the Lord's servants—that's us King's kids— Paul says, "Those who oppose him he must gently instruct, in the hope that God will grant them repentance leading them to a knowledge of the truth, and that they will come to their senses and escape from the trap of the devil, who has taken them captive to do his will" (NIV).

It's encouraging to think that maybe the Lord is using these tough situations in training the other guy as well as myself.

I'm learning to incorporate some of my learning about unpaid loans in a prayer that goes like this:

Lord Jesus, all that money that folks keep refusing to pay me is actually Your money, so the problem is actually Yours and no longer mine. Therefore, Lord, if this is the best You can do about Your money, then that's just fine with me. But if You can do better, then You just go ahead and cause those folks to send Your money to me. I'll deposit it to our bank account and write checks on it to support Your work in which You so graciously allow me to take part.

Lord, I just can't handle this mess, and if You can't,

that makes two of us. But Lord, just do the best You can with me and all those other folks, and I'll give You all the glory.

Did you pray the prayer with me? I have a hunch that if we pray in that manner every time we find ourselves about to burn up about those "good Christians" who owe us money, it may help.

That's known as "casting all your care upon him; for he careth for you" (1 Peter 5:7). Highly recommended.

All these are situations in which I seem to be still on "hold" in God's design. The position isn't comfortable; it isn't one I'd choose in a world run rampant with inflation; but others who are in the same boat with me agree that it's an unprecedented learning opportunity (understatement of the year!).

"Lord, send the money soon—I could use it—but meanwhile, don't let me goof up what You're doing in it all. Stay in charge, please."

The situation hasn't improved, but some days I don't even think about all those greenbacks. That, my friends, has to prove that God's in full charge of my pocketbook! And some days, He seems to multiply what's in it. It's okay if He doesn't, though. I just know He has some purpose—for me or the other persons—that He's working out in my "for the time being" straitened circumstances—even if "for the time being" turns out to be forever.

Have I totally succeeded in all that I'm supposed to do in these matters for best results this side of heaven? Not at all, but I'm getting better at it. At least, I no longer *always* get sweaty palms and a dry throat whenever I think about it. That has to be progress.

To wind this up, you'd rather be the robbed than the robber, wouldn't you? You're learning your lessons now—the other folks' are yet to come.

So bless you, my debtors, and thanks for the teaching!

PRINCIPLE: "Give to everyone who asks you [but not *all* he asks for], and if anyone takes what belongs to you, do not demand it back.... And if you lend to those from whom you expect repayment, what credit is that to you? Even 'sinners' lend to 'sinners,' expecting to be repaid in full. But love your enemies, do good to them, and lend to them without expecting to get anything back. Then your reward will be great . . . " (Luke 6:30, 34, 35 NIV).

8

Taming the Tongue—Again?

In several of my previous books, O Theophilus (the name means "lover of God," so I presume that applies to you, too), I have reported on how God healed me of colitis and ulcers and intestinal disorders when I stopped bad-mouthing others and began praising God that He could do anything at all with such imperfect things as people, especially me. And I talked a lot about such Scriptures as Proverbs 18:8, which gives a guaranteed method for developing a king-sized set of the above ailments by squirting the poison of tongue wagging about others and thereby receiving the undesirable effects within our own body's chemistry.

God puts it in these words: "The words of a talebearer are as wounds, and they go down into the innermost parts of the belly." As I understand anatomy, the ailments called ulcers, colitis, and intestinal flu happen in locations that are about as "innermost" as you can get.

Knowing all the truth—and teaching it—about how our bodies are programmed to react to the use of our tongues, I find I can still fall into the trap of negative reactions toward other people, and experience the drastic, disastrous, "innermost" results. It is amazing how many times God has to get my attention about these things!

Is it that I "lose my healing"? No, of course not. I simply take on another batch of ailments through a renewed anger kick, caused, of course, by my highly legitimate righteous indignation.

Funny thing about righteous indignation. Whether it is legitimate or not, it can kill you.

For several years I had not been bothered by any of these inner ailments, which used to be standard equipment with me until I turned my gossipy, bad-mouthing, poison-squirting tongue over to Jesus and He began to tame it with His powerful Holy Spirit ministry.

Then came the critical financial experience which made inner ailments a small price to pay—at first—for the luxury of bad-mouthing a fellow Christian who did me a dirty trick. Have you ever felt you would rather die than forgive someone for his unchristian behavior toward a nice person like you?

Don't pretend to be shocked. People make such choices all the time. The hospitals and graveyards are full of them, since such choices are generally terminal if they last long enough.

Anyhow, that's the way it was with me. Oh, I seethed!

How dare this respected Christian brother swindle me out of all those thousands of dollars? I'd get even with him! I'd bad-mouth him to the brethren. Well, I began to do it, and found—not to my surprise—that most of them were willing to joyfully join me in the bad-mouthing. My, but it was delicious!

We knew the Bible recommended that we pray for him, but how can you pray for somebody who refuses for months, turning into years, to give you a straight answer as to when he will repay all those thousands you advanced him when he was needy?

It's not easy.

Maybe you begin by praying, "Lord, fix *him* so he can't enjoy another decent night's sleep, so he won't digest a single mouthful of food, so his wife won't even *speak* to him until he does what's right and gives me my money."

With that kind of prayer, naturally I proceeded to develop those familiar old-time inner symptoms of burning ulcers, heartburn, and intestinal flu. You remember, don't you, that the causative factors for intestinal flu have never been isolated in the laboratory as "germs" or "viruses," because they're "bugs" developed when we're "bugged" by other people's behavior and our destructive attitudes toward them? If you don't remember, there's a refresher course in *How to Live in High Victory.*

While I was hurting, I was wailing, "Lord, it's *Your* money at stake! Why don't You do something about it?"

It was awfully quiet upstairs, but I seemed to catch the faintest whisper in my subconscious: *Aren't you showing some evidence that Hill's in charge here instead of Me?*

"But Lord, that money could be used for Your work in so many places if You could only get it released so I could use it for Your glory," I complained.

But Hill, if it's really My money, what on earth are you *complaining about?*

He had me there. It was the truth. Whenever I'm complaining about something or criticizing someone, that's a sure sign that I'm on the Throne of Judgment alongside God, trying to help Him sentence the brethren. So far in my experience, God never needs or wants that.

"Okay, Lord," I agreed, kind of reluctantly. "You take over then, and do what You can about this problem. I give up." I really meant it. "And I'll quit bad-mouthing him, too." It seemed a necessary afterthought, though it was a real sacrifice.

Once again, my inner ailments are disappearing, and peace like a river is flooding my soul most of the time. What about the money? Well, that's a different story.

The first penny has yet to show up, and the brother still evades my questions about his intentions. But if God is really in charge here—and I've given Him permission to be—the outcome is assured, in God's own time and way, and without ulcers, arthritis, colitis, or other reaction-related ailments in my seventy-five-year-old body which can do so much better without all that garbage.

In the interim, at this stage of my King's-kid life, I'm having many opportunities to learn to praise God for who He is instead of what He'll do for me. I must have needed to learn that—and learn it, and learn it—or God wouldn't have kindly given me so many lessons about it and, in the process, taught me to respect the other fellow's right to be wrong. God doesn't force men into righteousness and right behavior, and I've found I can't do it, either. They still have free will, an important part of God's overall plan for us in learning how to let God be God.

PRINCIPLE: "If you are convinced that you are a guide for the blind, a light for those who are in the dark, an instructor of the foolish, a teacher of infants, because you have in the law the embodiment of knowledge and truth—you, then, who teach others, do you not teach yourself?" (Romans 2:19–21 NIV).

9

Beans—and Being Booted Out

Did you detect a slight tinge of victory in the failures reported in the preceding chapter? Did it make you think things would eventually turn out all right, proving God was in charge of the goings-on while my pocketbook was getting skinnier and skinnier?

I've had a couple of other experiences lately, *not* in the financial department, where I detected some similar behind-the-scenes victories when what was out front looked like smashing failure. As a matter of fact, the first one involved a real, honest-to-goodness smashup on the highway.

It was September 22, 1980, a simply beautiful day, as my partner, Liz Rogers, and I drove through the farmlands of Indiana. "Little Sadie," my new Mercedes diesel, was purring along like a kitten knee-deep in whipping cream. The cassette tape to which we were listening had to do with God's love and mercy, and my mood was one of *yea* and *amen* and *thank You, Jesus.* It was a great day to be alive as kids of the King of the Universe.

Suddenly my vision was distracted from the peaceful two-lane country road stretching out ahead of me through lush farming country. I picked up the vibration of a roaring motor, and all at once my rearview mirror was filled with the ugly front end of a huge Peterbilt tractor-trailer about to climb right up onto Little Sadie's backside.

Before I could react at all, there was a mighty jolt from behind us as that monster crashed into the rear of my car. My cruise control was set on fifty-five miles an hour, which meant that the tractor had been traveling considerably faster.

As the attacker began to slow down, so did I, and the pair of us came to a shaky stop a few hundred yards farther down the road. Climbing out and comparing notes, we learned that the driver of the truck had apparently dozed at the wheel and crashed into my trunk, where his license bracket had done many hundreds of dollars worth of damage to my brand-new, beautiful Mercedes. Poor Little Sadie. And the twenty tons of green beans with which the truck was loaded assured me that except for the grace of God, things could have added up to total disaster.

Why did it happen to us? Hadn't we been out on God's work, fulfilling our part of the Great Commission? Hadn't I been speaking for His glory on a program with Lester Sumrall just that morning in South Bend? And hadn't I bragged about Jesus on Channel 38 in Chicago just a couple of days before? And what about our laboring in His vineyard at Glory Village in Chesterton, Indiana, the previous four days? Didn't that entitle us to His protection?

These thoughts, laments, murmurings, and pity-party ruminations came tumbling through my head for an instant, only to be stopped when my gears shifted to what I should have been wondering about from the first, the point of view that's always a winning attitude: "Lord, what's in this for You?"

Once I had shifted gears, He began to show me what He saw from His great, loving outlook in eternity. Frankly, it blew my mind.

Here was a young man, driving his own tractor-trailer rig from the farm to the cannery, having gotten up before daybreak and worked laboriously in order to get to the cannery while the beans were still fresh. No one would have faulted him for taking a much-needed siesta after lunch. There was nothing wrong with a little nap. Of course the time and place could have been improved upon.

Ahead on the highway lay a little country town with a single main street lined with parked vehicles. A few children were happily at play out in the middle of things. If Little Sadie and I hadn't been right where we were to impede the progress of that monster beanbag, the driver would have continued his afternoon snooze right into the middle of town, probably knocking down kids like tenpins as he hurtled several episodes of death and destruction into the local populace.

The impact of his front end crashing into my back end must have been good—it woke him up just in time to avoid all sorts of tragedy.

The moment I realized all that, I praised God for giving me the privilege of being His instrument to effect such a deliverance!

Later, when I told someone about my experience, his reaction was, "Well, if you had been hearing the voice of the Lord that day, it wouldn't have happened!" That, of course, echoed the normal, commonsense outlook of a carnal-minded Christian, which is no different from a once-born pagan. But I'm not sure he was all that right. A King's kid is always aware that there is a way to accept *all* things—whatever happens—in the light of Romans 8:28 when there is no opportunity to change them on the spot through the gifts of the Spirit. In this case, it all happened so fast, there was no time for changing anything except my attitude. The insurance company paid for the damage to the vehicles, and no one was injured. I didn't even get a whiplash.

Was God in charge there? No question about it. Things

worked out better than if it hadn't happened, all things considered, because here I am telling you about it and strengthening your faith with a fresh word of testimony. I was able to give a testimony to the highway patrolman, the insurance company, and the fellow at the body shop, too.

It was a clear case of taking a situation that could have spelled GLOP—I mean, we could have had bean soup and babies all over the highway—and adding one more ingredient, Jesus, to literally turn it all into glory.

(Do you see how that works? Christ is abbreviated in Greek by the symbol X, called "Chi" in the Greek language. You take the lower right quadrant of the X and attach it to a P, making it an R, and what you have left is a Y. GLOP becomes GLORY—because He has redeemed the world. I stay excited about things like that because I know that when He's in charge, that's the normal order of things.)

There are times, I must confess, when it's a little less comfortable to be His agent. Take the time a few weeks before the tractor-trailer incident, for example.

I had been invited to be the Friday-night and Saturday-afternoon speaker at a convention. The invitation had asked that I come and share my personal testimony.

Sister Liz Rogers, my partner in the King's Kids' Korner ministry, and I had driven down together from Baltimore, she to man the King's Kids' Korner book table with my books and tapes and upside-down I AM A KING'S KID pins, which is her ministry, and I to do my usual bragging about Jesus.

(In case you hadn't heard, the I AM A KING'S KID pin is *made* upside down—by an exclusive patented process—so people will notice it and ask why. "So was I until Jesus turned me right side up," you can grin at them. It's a perfect opener for your testimony.)

The brother who chaired the meeting seemed under great stress as we sat down to eat. After a sumptuous dinner, several of us filed into the prayer room for surrender of the meeting to the Lord, which took it out of our hands and placed it where it belonged—in the nail-scarred hands of Jesus. But the tension seemed to mount throughout the preliminaries of the evening.

Then came my turn to speak, and for the next hour and a half, as the Lord led, I was not surprised to find the message slanting in the direction of Romans 8:28, coupled with 3 John 2–4.

"God wants heaven's best in our lives," I assured the audience, "but to be in line to receive it, we must allow certain things to be removed from our experience." I heard myself speaking with great conviction, and from there on, if I had stuck to the spiritual side of things, talking about "Be ye holy; for I am holy," as Peter quoted it from Leviticus (1 Peter 1:16), I'd probably have been on safe ground. But I got practical, you might say, and began to talk about how, many times, our prayers for healing are not answered because we carry around too many pounds of lard on our frames, which is not heaven's best, healthwise.

Pointing out a problem isn't too helpful unless you tell the brethren how to get rid of it, so I proceeded to let the listeners in on the contents of my book *How to Flip Your Flab—Forever,* in which I explain how God lifted thirty-six pounds off me in thirty-six weeks and has kept them off my formerly flabbo waistline for over two years till now.

Then the Lord brought to my mind, for sharing, something I had read in *Sugar Blues* about the results of refined sugar and white flour in the diets of people who are King's kids and who are not King's kids. It is a startling fact that sugar turns out to be a highly addictive drug when it encounters our body chemistry. It literally becomes an obsessive spirit or demon, demanding that we eat more and more of it. If you've ever tried to say no to a piece of candy or a gloppy dessert, you know how addictive it is.

After dealing with the two chief offenders—refined sugar and white flour—and recommending that they be scratched from the list of acceptable foods for King's kids who want the best in the health department for their temples of the Holy Spirit, I zeroed in on Romans 8:28 as the recommended theme song for King's kids. It's just another way of saying that God's in charge here, in all circumstances, for good.

I ended my part of the program by encouraging each one present to be a believer in action according to Mark 16:17 by laying hands on one another, and expecting healing to follow.

I had just barely said the *amen* at the end of our corporate prayer when the lightning hit the privy, as the old-time saying goes.

Chairman shot out of his seat with the most demonic expression on his face I have ever seen. He was literally spewing hatred from every cell of his being.

"You were not in the Spirit, brother!" he roared, for all to hear. "Everything you said was in the flesh, and you've ruined the whole meeting!" He was shouting at the top of his lungs right there in front of the entire nine hundred brethren, who stood aghast at this unexpected outbreak of hate, anger, and bad manners.

I was so taken by surprise that I stood speechless for a few moments, my jaw hanging loose, almost unhinged. Quite an experience for old Motor-mouth Hill.

Then, before I could utter a word, Chairman continued squirting vindictive venom: "I'm taking you off the program for tomorrow afternoon! I'm canceling your talk at my church Sunday morning!" By then, he was livid and white by turns, and I feared for his blood vessels, to say nothing of his sanity.

Finally I regained my composure and managed to squeak out, "But brother, I spoke as the Lord led, which is what I always do—"

"You did no such thing! That was all of the flesh! You're to have no further part in the weekend activities!"

"Brother," I begged, completely mystified as to what had set him off, "please tell me what I said that—"

"All that talk about sugar and flour! These people aren't ready to hear such things!"

So that was it. I had tromped all over Satan's favorite approach system, and he was furious. In all my years of speaking at these affairs, I had never received such treatment. Having been thrown out of conferences several times over the years for introducing people to the Baptism in the Holy Spirit, now I was adding a new thing to my "Reasons for Eviction" list, and a new place to my "Places I Have Been Thrown Out Of" list.

Then began the battle. Old Slue Foot donned his long red underwear and tried to get me to retract my own very persuasive teaching from Romans 8:28. I had to remind myself of the handle of that verse, "*And we know* that all things work together for good . . ." (my italics). Not because it looks good or feels good, but because God's Word says He's going to work it for good, anyway.

Everything within me cried out for the right "just this once" to make exceptions to that doctrine and crank up a first-class pity party.

"But Lord! He's guilty of rebuking an elder! In front of all those people! He's only seven years old in the Spirit, and here he is, just a young punk, working me over—in front of everybody! Lord, I'm in my twenty-sixth year of serving

You!" I reminded Him of all my virtues, just in case He had forgotten.

Silence from heaven.

Turning to the second in command of the convention, I asked him, "Are you going to allow this to happen—to let him fire me from the program when I've come all the way from Baltimore?" I still couldn't believe it.

Mr. Second in Command shrugged. "Chairman is the head man around here, and what he says is what we do."

I wanted to say something sarcastic about what a dictatorship that was. I wanted to tell them I was quitting the whole lousy mess—forever. I wanted to tell them I'd report them to the international office. But I didn't say anything more—out loud. Inside, I pouted like a two-year-old. "I'll pack my bags and go home, and *then* they'll be sorry."

But Chairman punctured that balloon when he insisted, "Of course we'll take proper care of you if you care to spend the weekend here." I wanted to take proper care of him with a hefty punch in the snout! But the Lord held me steady.

I thanked Chairman for his hospitality—almost choking to death on the words—and said I would enjoy being a convener for a change instead of someone up front. Then, though I nearly swallowed my Adam's apple, I stayed, publicly humiliated before the entire convention, fired from the program, and literally rejected the rest of the weekend by the top management.

Some of the brethren seemed apologetic when Chairman wasn't looking, and the enemy kept trying to shove me into open warfare, but every time I was about to explode with another "justificating" thought about how right I was and how wrong Chairman was, the Lord came on strong with an inner reminder: *I'm in charge here. Let Me handle it.* And I'd simmer down and let God be God.

It wasn't easy, but I sat at the book table and autographed

books for the few folks who were brave enough to venture near me. Some asked what had happened, and I simply told them I had been fired from the program for reasons satisfactory to the Chairman.

When the Saturday-afternoon session opened, with someone else speaking in my place, I listened and was greatly blessed. Scuttlebutt got to me that some persons had left the convention after the sorry (that's Southern for "second best") Friday-night affair, muttering, "Even pagans don't treat each other that way. I think I'll stick with my religion."

At the end of the Saturday-evening session, at which twelve hundred or more had gathered for what was to have been a great healing service but didn't quite turn out that way, Chairman thanked all the speakers for coming—except me, of course—and invited everyone to visit the book tables—except mine, of course—and I was squashed underfoot once again.

"Lord!" I howled, pausing from licking my wounds. "Can't I please say just one word in my defense? Don't I have the right as a mature Christian to put these young upstarts in their place?"

Before I could get on my feet to holler, "Now hear this! Thus saith the Lord—" He stopped me.

Yes, Hill, you have a right as a mature Christian—to pray for these younger ones.

Well, if He wouldn't let me get even here, I'd get even when I got home. I'd write them a letter so hot—and when they responded in kind, I'd burn their letter without reading it. *That* would fix 'em!

After I got home, I wrote four letters—and didn't mail a single one. Then, with the poison letters out of my system, the Lord dictated one that said what He wanted me to say. It went like this:

Thank you, Chairman, for your help and cooperation at the convention in providing a book table for the King's Kids' Korner ministry. And thank you for your hospitality in feeding and bedding-down facilities. And thanks most of all for a brand-new experience, that of being publicly fired from your program before nine hundred-odd people. Wow! I had no idea I needed that, but if Romans 8:28 means anything, God will do something wonderful with it, and so I thank you for it. We are praying for you.

Gradually, in such bits and pieces as I could absorb and digest, the Lord began showing me how He was giving me opportunities to identify with His own experience of rejection for the sake of truth. He made me realize that if we are on His team, we can expect persecution to increase. There was the further Word that when these things begin to happen, King's kids are to "look up... for your redemption draweth nigh" (Luke 21:28). I think that's God's own way of saying, "Hang in there, baby, and I'll make it all turn out just right."

Is God going to work all things together for good in that humiliation for me? No question about it! His Word says He will do it.

How? In what way could He be glorified through such carryings-on? It's none of my business to check God's ways and means in other people's lives. My assignment is to let Him be God in my life and in everyone else's life at the same time and for the same reason: We don't know what the Lord is doing, but we know He's doing something, and it's for our good. God is sovereign God, in charge of our mountaintops as well as of our valleys, if we will only believe it.

In this case, my educated idiot box told me, "Chairman certainly quenched the Spirit right out of that meeting and it fell flatter than a pancake," and I relayed the message to the Lord.

Then along came several people who wrote, telling me how my testimony had blessed them. For some reason, they hadn't even heard the rhubarb.

Could it be that some might have gotten the no-sugar message more forcibly into their gizzards *because* of the great opposition?

Maybe I needed to be humbled.

Maybe Chairman needed the prayers of the saints who surely prayed for him after that violent display.

Maybe God was working out something for someone who was not even on the platform.

There was probably lots of good, once you started looking for it.

Even while I was still licking my wounds, He began to change my tune from, "Oh, it's not an easy road," to "Praise God, I'm *on* the road!" Whether I get hit by flying beanbags or flying furies, I've decided it's all worth the trip, when I let Him be in charge here. What a relief to simply let God be God—in Chairman's life as well as my own.

PRINCIPLE: "Blessed are you when people insult you, persecute you and falsely say all kinds of evil against you because of me. Rejoice and be glad, because great is your reward in heaven, for in the same way they persecuted the prophets who were before you" (Matthew 5:11, 12 NIV).

10

Of Evidence and Eyeballs

Are you ready now to talk about healings that haven't happened? Let's begin with a simple case history.

More than twelve years ago, in a laboratory experiment, I burned a hole completely through the retina of my left eye, making that eyeball legally blind. (You can read about the original catastrophe in *How to Live in High Victory* and an interim updating in *Instant Answers for King's Kids in Training.*)

After it happened, I prayed, of course, asking the God who had made the eye in the first place to fix it up as good as new. I knew He was able to do that, because He had given me a new spinal disk right after I first got saved. (That's in *How to Live Like a King's Kid.*)

When nothing happened after my own eyeball prayers, many other people prayed for me, so many I lost count. But my eyeball didn't get healed. Did that mean that something was wrong with their faith? Or mine? Or that there was evil hidden in our hearts? Were we impatient or unforgiving? Had we somehow "missed God"?

Maybe none of these things were true—maybe all of them were true. God's the only One who knows. In the meantime, I learned a lot from the different approaches laid on me by the brethren who prayed for me. Want to hear a few? They amount to a whole encyclopedia of the doctrines of men, all of them missing the mark of truth.

One fellow said, "Now, brother, when I repeat the Word of God, 'By His stripes I'm healed,' just receive your sight." I tried. Nothing happened. But the pray-er seemed perfectly satisfied that now I could see perfectly without my glasses. But he was perfectly wrong.

Another brother prayed a really loud and highly confident prayer, assuring me afterward, "God cannot lie." Then he added this tidbit: "You get what you say," trying to put the blame on me if it didn't happen according to his program. But I was too smart for that. I cooperated. "Thank You, Jesus, for my perfect vision," I said. But I didn't get what I said. "The healer" disappeared into the woodwork somewhere, and I left the prayer meeting as blind as ever.

Still another brother of considerable renown for his mighty prowess in prayer told me, "If your own prayers were doing you any good, you wouldn't be asking me to pray for you, so from now on, say nothing, do nothing." Glad to be obedient to anybody who might get better results than I had gotten, I stopped thanking Jesus and just went about my business, leaving my praying to him. My eye didn't change.

One more brother took a different approach. He told me just to stand still and receive my healing. While I acted like a statue, he laid hands on me and shouted with enough decibels to shatter the crockery for miles around, "It is finished! Just act like it! The healing is yours by inheritance, brother! It's part of the atonement! Hallelujah!"

I hallelujahed with him, and it sounded great. He was deliriously happy, but my eyeball seemed to ignore the whole thing. I was still legally blind in my left eye.

Anointing oil? I've had enough of it applied to my left eye

and its environs to float a battleship. All that is quite scriptural (James 5:14, 15), but I'm *still* blind in my left eye.

How come?

I dunno.

For a while, I went around saying, "I'm healed by the stripes of Jesus," to anyone who asked me about my eye. When they looked puzzled, I shifted gears and went into double-talk to explain that the fact that, for all practical purposes, I was still blind as a bat in that eye, meant only that my healing hadn't manifested itself yet. This kind of idiocy made me uncomfortable, and I saw it didn't do other people much good either. Pagans got turned off right away, shaking their heads and muttering something about "roof trouble" every time they cast their eyes in my direction.

One day it occurred to me that the lie of Christian Science—mind over matter—had subtly crept into the Charismatic movement without its label. I saw, too, that Webster's definition of healing would include the manifestation—restoration of my eyesight to its original sound condition—so I stopped my double-talk, refused to rewrite the dictionary, and started to be as honest as I knew how to be.

"Yes," I began to say to inquirers, "I accidentally shot the retina out of my left eye a dozen years ago, so I'm legally blind in that eye—20/195. But I've asked God to heal it, and I'm believing the healing will show up where I can see it any day now, in whatever 'the fullness of time' happens to be in this case."

That caused some to shake their heads in wonder at the faith they saw in me, but it didn't slam the door on my testimony. Some even said, kind of longingly, "I wish I had a faith like that!" opening the door for me to tell them where to get it. When they responded in a positive manner, it was well worth the 20/195.

Could it be that God is using even a burned-out eyeball, working it for good in His scheme of things?

Somewhere along the way, one of the biggies in the healing ministry issued an edict which goes like this: "If a Christian is right with God, he will never experience tragedy in his life."

What a wicked guilt trip that is to lay on somebody already burdened with blindness or deafness, to someone grieving over the loss of a loved one, or to a patient in a hospital.

The Job syndrome—and that's what that is—was a doctrine of men that God had to dispel among Job's brethren as well as among the disciples who wanted to lay the blame on somebody for the man born blind. One brother actually hinted it was that way with my loss of vision. "Hidden sin, brother," was his diagnosis, and since he couldn't further enlighten me, he didn't improve the situation. I was glad not to have to listen to him a second time.

I understand that someone told Oral Roberts that the death of his loved ones in a plane crash was due to hidden sins in his own life. How unloving and condemning can you get?

The plain truth is that because Adam chose second best in the Garden of Eden, we live on a cursed planet. Under those circumstances, bad things are bound to happen—to the just and unjust alike—regardless of what I or any other "faith teacher" says to the contrary.

More smelling salts, anybody? While you're regaining consciousness, think about it. The Bible says in many places—even in the New Testament—that tribulation of one kind or another can be expected, *even by King's kids,* during our sojourn on Planet Earth. He wouldn't have told us to count our trials all joy (James 1:2) if we weren't going to have any trials, would He?

There's another unscriptural guilt trip to be considered here, tied in with the occasion when a great prayer warrior told me, "Brother, if you have been prayed for more than once for that eye ailment, you are showing lack of faith." This, of course, made me feel worse than ever, because by that time I had been prayed for without ceasing (1 Thessalonians 5:17) by many dozens of folks. Still others had kept on asking, seeking, and knocking, according to the clear directions of other Scriptures (Matthew 7:7 AMPLIFIED). And then there was that perfect lesson in the experience of Jesus, as recounted in Mark 8:22–25, where He Himself, the Lord of glory, administered eyeball healing on the installment plan. Apparently the doctrines of men were wrong again!

Praise God for the Scriptures that say He's in charge, no matter what men may say!

Well, after many scores of heavy-, medium-, and light-duty prayers by persons of all kinds of doctrinal persuasions, I got to the point where Paul must have found himself after praying about his thorn in the flesh three different times (2 Corinthians 12:8). I decided to go back to the foundation fact of the Christian life and begin to praise God for who He is instead of what He might be talked into doing for me. Then I cast all my cares about my eye on Him. My prayer went something like this:

"Lord, You do the caring for me and my affliction. I've cared enough about it already, to the point of totally giving up. Paul said he was going to take pleasure in his infirmities for Christ's sake, and I'm going to do it, too. If You can't do anything about the infirmity of my unseeing eyeball, that makes a whole bunch of us, so it's all Yours."

That detaching from ownership of the problem, I remembered, lined up with the first point of Jesus' Sermon on the Mount, where He assured us that the poor in spirit are blessed, because the kingdom of heaven belongs to them (Matthew 5:3).

Did anything happen after that prayer? Not immediately, as far as cataclysmic evidence was concerned. As a matter of fact, I kind of forgot about my need for healing in the eye department. I thanked God for my bifocals, which I needed for driving as well as reading, because I couldn't see anything clearly without them. A couple of times over the years, when things got blurry, I went back to the eye doctor and got a new prescription, then forked over sixty or eighty simoleons of the Lord's money for new spectacles, with no feelings of guilt, and praised Him for being in full charge even though the evidence of my five senses couldn't pick up any improvement in my vision.

When a well-meaning brother here or there suggested that my lack of faith was the reason for my glasses, I thanked him for his interest and went on thanking God, too. I probably should have given the fellow some Scriptures that showed Bible healings where the sick person didn't even know what faith was, much less have a basketful, but I didn't. "If any man be ignorant, let him be ignorant" (1 Corinthians 14:38), I said, just as Paul did. Respecting someone else's right to be wrong is important to me. In fact, it's a lifesaver sometimes.

Years went by, and then one night something happened. While on a family vacation at Christian Retreat in Bradenton, Florida, Liz Rogers received a word of knowledge from the Lord: *I'm going to heal Hal's eyes . . . you pray.*

Because the word came to her so unexpectedly one night during the evening message, Liz asked the Lord for a confirmation, whereupon the speaker stopped in mid-sentence, made spectacles with his fingers, and shouted loudly, "Do you see?"

From that time until the Lord lifted the burden from her heart, Liz interceded in prayer daily. And God hastened His word to perform it.

How did that work out in my experience? Read on.

I was standing in the pulpit of the Church of the Good Shepherd, in Maitland, Florida, to minister the Word and share my experiences with the brethren. As I looked out over the congregation, everything seemed so indistinct and hazy that I suspected my specs needed a bath. I took them off and began wiping them of what I guessed must have been at least an inch-thick layer of sludge from an exploding oil well that had somehow escaped my notice. Before I propped the cheaters back on my nose, I happened to glance up and out over the assembled congregation.

Lo, and behold, the people weren't blurry! I could see them!

The healing of my distant vision had happened in the twinkling of an eye. While the results had appeared in an instant of time, after I had forgotten all about my ailment, God was faithful to answer the prayer that He himself had given to Liz. My imperfect eyeball could have served its purpose, whatever it was, and the sovereignty of God had brought into evidence, in the fullness of time, one segment of what I'm trusting will be a complete healing—on the in-stallment plan.

All that happened three years ago, and I haven't needed glasses for driving or normal day-to-day functioning since then. But I still have to wear them for reading fine print.

Why does the God who is all perfection allow healing to come in installments? I dunno. Will God eventually give me 20/20 vision in that injured eye? I can't tell you. He's in charge here. If and when He sees fit to install 20/20 vision in the injured organ, I'm primed to give Him all the glory. In the meantime, I've quit pretending I have perfect vision when the evidence is clear I don't. When He's in charge, I don't have to lie for Him. He has a reason for everything He does, and as far as I'm concerned, His timing is better than mine could ever be.

Now, I have a friend Tom who had an eye adventure very different from mine. Tom was attending a meeting where J. A. Dennis was ministering. After the service, Tom went up to the front to give Mr. Dennis a hearty handshake and to thank Him for his good message. Brother Dennis took one look at Tom, reached up and lifted Tom's powerful bifocals off his nose, folded them up, and tucked them into Tom's pocket, saying to him, "You won't need them anymore." And sure enough, he hasn't.

Why wasn't the healing of my eye according to the pattern God followed in Tom's case? I dunno. Furthermore, it's none of my business. We can't make a doctrine out of how God worked one time and require Him to follow that method forever after. If we could, we'd punch it all into a computer and would never again have to seek the Lord at all. Whenever we had a problem, we'd just push the button with the right label. It's good God doesn't let us get by with something like that.

Someone has described the Christian life as "living loose in Jesus," and I kind of like that. It seems to work.

Before I forget it, there was an interesting little sidelight on all this eye business. During the time my injury was being checked by the Maryland State Labor Board as an industrial accident coming under its jurisdiction, my daughter, Linda, learned that the home she was renting was on the market to be sold, so she had to find another place to live on quite short notice.

We all prayed about it, of course, and as the deadline approached, a highly desirable house became available. All the details were ideal—except for the money. Linda had to come up almost immediately with a considerable sum of cash for a down payment, and she didn't have it. Just as all doors closed, and it appeared that the purchase couldn't go through, my insurance company sent me a check for my damaged eyeball—which just happened to be the exact amount Linda needed for the house.

It hadn't occurred to any of us that God was using my eye injury, in His overall plan for our lives, to make possible the purchase of a home for Linda, but He did it anyhow.

By praying and interceding "in secret" before the Lord, instead of bragging to the world what she was up to, Liz focused the Holy Spirit prayer power where it belonged. Her actions were in line with the instructions in Matthew 6:1–6 TLB:

> Take care! Don't do your good deeds publicly, to be admired, for then you will lose the reward from your Father in heaven. . . . But when you do a kindness to someone, do it secretly. . . . And your Father who knows all secrets will reward you. . . . But when you pray, go away by yourself, all alone, and shut the door behind you and pray to your Father secretly, and your Father, who knows your secrets, will reward you.

That could be a helpful hint to others who have wondered why their prayers have apparently fallen on deaf ears. Maybe what's needed sometimes is a little less "Now hear this!" and a little more "Shhhh!"

Time for a bottom line again.

Lots of times God heals in answer to prayer. Lots of times He doesn't. Why? Sometimes we suspect there's unforgiveness, impatience, or unbelief—the three big roadblocks (you can read more about them in *How to Live Like a King's Kid*)—but in the vast majority of cases, the truth is simply, "I dunno."

But we do know this—whether healing happens, or doesn't happen, God's in charge here.

PRINCIPLE: "... In this world you will have trouble. But take heart! I have overcome the world" (John 16:33 NIV).

11

More Failure

Let's see now. We're about ten chapters along. Are you sufficiently conditioned to hear about some *real* failures? Hold on to your hats. Here they come.

In all these years of talking about King's-kid living, praying for thousands of folks, and watching others pray for more thousands, I have yet to see a real wheelchair patient get up and walk. Not one.

That's hard to believe, isn't it? I mean, you'd think they'd get up right and left just because I asked God to heal them, wouldn't you. So would I, but it just hasn't happened for me—or for anybody else when I was watching them.

How come? To hear me talk, you'd have thought I certainly had enough faith for it, wouldn't you? And that I understood all the principles involved well enough that if it could have happened for anybody, it could have happened for Hill the Healer?

I don't even like to think about it. But the only way I can change the subject is to report some failures of a different variety—a trio of reports you'll find hard to believe, coming from me.

First, Bob (none of these names are real, but the people are, and what happened to them) had been completely delivered from alcohol-and-drug addiction and was back in his profession of computer programming, though he was still suffering from occasional deep depressions. One night, in desperation, he came to our prayer group, gave his life to Jesus, and for months lived a highly victorious Christian life. Then the pressure of his business life became intolerable, and he took "just one small tranquilizer" because his doctor assured him it was perfectly safe.

It wasn't. There is often an unrealized half-life principle built into these drugs, whereby a bad return "trip" may take place if additional ingestion ever occurs. It happened to Bob. The day after taking the "perfectly harmless" tranquilizer, he was again deep into the suicidal manic-depressive state from which Jesus had totally delivered him.

We got the prayer power going again, of course, and did everything possible to effect another deliverance. But in this case, it was apparently "one to a customer, please." Nothing worked. Instead, everything got worse. We prayed in the Spirit, and we prayed with the understanding, all to no avail. We exhorted the demon spirits to leave Bob, but they pretended to be asleep.

A few nights later, he telephoned to say that the lying demon spirits had ordered him to shoot himself. Some members of the prayer fellowship rushed over to stay with him around the clock in an effort to bridge the chasm of obvious mental incompetence.

The next day, during a lapse in the close attention being given him by concerned friends and loved ones, Bob shot himself.

Jack, the second case, was an early leader of the spiritual-life fellowship in Baltimore and totally dedicated to serving Jesus. As far as I could see, he lived out his dedication in all areas of his life, and was a real example to me as I entered into this new dimension back in 1954.

Then something happened which we couldn't identify, but we could see the results of it. Jack began to criticize the organized church and to spread the false story that God had finished with it, and we should therefore "come out from among them" (2 Corinthians 6:17), leave it, and shake the dust off our feet. That was his opinion, nowhere taught in the Bible as we understood it, and we could all sense the dampening of the action of the Spirit in our prayer meetings when Jack was present. No one was surprised when a short time later we learned that he had fallen into a cult.

Zealous newcomers, like yours truly, took Jack on as a prayer project, asking God daily to "turn his crooked paths into straight ones." We asked God to bring him back to teaching the truth of the Bible and to leave off the hare-brained schemes and "foolosophies" of fallible men.

Our prayer words were right and proper, but our spirits were so critical that instead of loosing him to Jesus we were, in effect, binding him to his error. In other words, because our hearts were not right toward him, we were actually "praying amiss" (*see* James 4:3).

Once we realized that, and saw our double-mindedness in wanting to blame him at the same time we were asking the Lord to bless him, we asked the Lord to do the praying for us. That way we wouldn't have a chance to mess our prayers up, and God could have His way. The next day, we heard these words come from our lips: "Lord, bring our Brother Jack's teaching into conformity with Your Word—or else take him home."

Two days later, Jack went into the hospital with a slight pain in his chest, and twenty-four hours later, Jesus took him home. The error into which he had fallen didn't have a chance to captivate anyone else in the fellowship. Later we learned it was the same error as that behind the Jonestown disaster, which was involved in the next case, also.

Chuck, a great religious leader of recent years, became involved in a cult that taught "sinless perfection." Soon he had gathered around him a group of people with "itching ears" (2 Timothy 4:3). He began assuring them that he was divine, and that his earthly body would never die.

"O Lord," we prayed, "please reveal to the world the falsity of Chuck's claims, and deliver him from the lying spirits which are deceiving him."

The next day, Chuck's private airplane crashed, and he was killed.

Were our prayers for Bob, Jack, and Chuck answered? Certainly not in the way we expected, a way that would have looked "good" to the world. But was God in charge? Could He have been using the bad examples to teach people to stick close to the Word of God and not be led off into any heretical side trips?

You find your own answers. I have mine. Would a "good" God let such things happen? Here's what the Word says:

PRINCIPLE: "They perish because they refused to love the truth and so be saved. For this reason God sends them a powerful delusion so that they will believe the lie and so that all will be condemned who have not believed the truth but have delighted in wickedness" (2 Thessalonians 2:10–12 NIV).

"But there were also false prophets among the people, just as there will be false teachers among you. They will secretly introduce destructive heresies, even denying the sovereign Lord who bought them—bringing swift destruction on themselves" (2 Peter 2:1 NIV).

12

The Rise of the Fall-Down Syndrome

All this is getting kind of gloomy, isn't it? Let's take a recess to insert a parenthetical chapter about a phenomenon taking place these days in many meetings of Charismatic Christians. The phenomenon is variously described as being "slain in the Spirit," or "falling under the power of God," and it works like this:

The healer, or evangelist, or whoever, gives an altar call for salvation, Baptism with the Holy Ghost, healing, or some other purpose. People flock forward to receive the ministry, and one by one, as the minister lays hands on them—or even merely points in their direction—the candidates for blessing keel over backward, as if in a dead faint.

Don't worry. They never get hurt because, aware that such a thing is likely to happen (counting on it, maybe?), the minister has already spoken to some of the more muscular men in the meeting and alerted them to be ready to step up and catch the keelers and help them land safely on the well-padded carpet. There may be additional persons alerted to cover the knees of keeled females with a little square cloth that serves as a kind of modesty token.

Because people are often disturbed by this fall-down syndrome, or domino reaction, as some call it, I've had many questions addressed to me about it. Here are some of them, with answers from the Manufacturer's Handbook. Know-

ing that people often perish for lack of knowledge, I'm in
favor of helping to dispel as much ignorance as possible.

1. *Is the phenomenon known as "slain in the Spirit" referred
to in the Bible?* I've looked, but have not found it in any of
the translations with which I am familiar.

2. *Does the Bible make any reference to God's people falling
under God's power?* Yes, there are such references, but in
every case I have examined, God's people are said to have
fallen on their faces before Him, not on their backs. I have
not been able to discover a single instance in which God's
people fell backward into the arms of a catcher.

3. *Didn't the Roman soldiers fall backward when they came
to arrest Jesus?* Apparently, but they were pagans, not
Christians, unless they were converted in that moment, and
I find no scriptural evidence that they were. Also, no
catchers are mentioned.

4. *But how about Paul?* Yes, he fell to the ground on the
Damascus Road, but it happened before he was converted.
In any case, no catcher is mentioned as part of the proce-
dure.

5. *Is it ever a true manifestation of the Holy Spirit when
people fall backward under the power of God?* God's the only
one who knows about that. I have no dogmatic answer to
that question, but I have observed that when God's in
charge, people will usually be blessed by what happens.
When He's not in charge, they might be turned off instead.
In my travels, I have encountered many newcomers who
confess to being puzzled, not blessed, by the fall-down syndrome.

6. *Have you ever experienced this phenomenon yourself,
Brother Hill?* Yes, on one occasion, I made myself fall down
to see what it felt like. Result? I felt foolish. But that's not to

say that you may be acting likewise if it happens to you. To each his own. No doctrines, remember?

7. *Is there any scientific parallel in the law of physics, as far as you know?* Yes, there is, and I find it quite interesting. Care to hear about it? (If you don't, you can skip down to number 8 below. No harm done.)

In an electrical power system, energy flows freely where no restriction exists in the circuit. God the Holy Spirit is like a power system. "Ye shall receive power" is the promise of Acts 1:8, and we do receive power when Jesus baptizes us in the Holy Spirit. (You can read all about that in *How to Live Like a King's Kid.*)

Reactions to this baptism are manifested in different ways. Some people shake, some laugh, some weep with joy, some fall to the floor in an out-of-this-world state and remain prone for a long period of time. In other folks, nothing visible takes place. Onlookers were not aware of the bath of liquid love that seemed to flow over me from head to foot, for instance, when Jesus baptized me in the Holy Spirit.

Why so many different reactions to the same Spirit? Is one experience indicative of more Spirit than another? When I asked Jesus about these things, He compared electrical circuits and Holy Spirit power circuits, that is, King's kids. It was very interesting. Let me explain.

When resistance is introduced into any electrical power circuit, it shows up in terms of a manifestation of energy. If the resistance is in the form of a light bulb, there will be a glow to indicate that power has been interrupted by the presence of resistance to the flow. If the resistance is in the form of a burner on an electric range, the glow will be accompanied by a considerable amount of heat. The greater the restriction, the greater the evidence of it.

In King's-kid circuits, the analog means that the greater

the resistance to the flow of the power of the Spirit, the greater will be the physical evidence of the power flow. Thus, if I have inner obstructions to the flow of the Spirit in me, I may well jump, jerk, twitch, wriggle, or roll over, depending on how much internal resistance there is to the free flow of Holy Spirit power through my total being.

(This does not necessarily have anything to do with any conscious resisting of God. It may mean that God is burning out my hangups with the Holy Ghost and with fire, as is mentioned in the Gospels in connection with this baptism that Jesus carries out in those who believe in Him.)

When God is in charge here, the manifestation—if any—is His doing, and the results are equally His business.

8. *Why does God do these things?* I dunno. I have no idea why God does a number of things the way He does them. And the fall-down syndrome, which has reached epidemic proportions in the last several years, is just one more thing about which I have to confess I'm not the final authority. God's in charge here.

9. *Is God always in this experience?* I dunno. I do know of others, besides myself, who confess that for reasons of their own—curiosity, perhaps, or to be spiritually fashionable—have made themselves fall down. Some say they had such a hefty assist from the minister that not to fall would have seemed a major breach of etiquette. Anyhow, in some circles, falling down is really the "in" thing to do, almost as popular as leg-lengthening was a while back, or as playing racquetball is in today's secular world.

In spite of its popularity, I was surprised in a recent meeting to be approached by a sweet Christian sister who was into these things in a big way.

"What is your need?" I asked her when she came up for prayer.

"Please pray for me to fall down," she said. "I have fallen down seven times already in other meetings."

Because I was knocked practically unconscious by the unexpectedness of her request, I can't report on what happened next. I wish I had had the presence of mind to ask if she was trying for the *Guinness Book of World Records,* but I didn't. It did occur to me on that occasion, however, that maybe things were getting a little out of hand. Keeping score of your fallings might be interesting, but so far, I can't find it in my Bible. And to my knowledge, Parker Brothers hasn't copyrighted any rule book on the subject, either.

(I did find *downsitting* and *uprising* in my Bible concordance. Psalms 139:2 says that God knows about them, although they don't sound nearly so dramatic as falling down.)

What's the bottom line about this fall-down syndrome? Here's a handy checklist of questions for *you* to answer about it and many other phenomena about which you may have wondered:

1. Does it glorify God—or make a spectacle of the one who keels over?
2. Do folks come into a closer walk with Jesus through this experience?
3. Are the unsaved brought into the kingdom of God when folks fall down?
4. Is anybody edified?
5. Is the keeler a better witness or a more faithful minister of the Word?
6. Is attention diverted from Jesus toward the center of fall-down activity?
7. Is the experience clearly taught in the Bible and unmistakably suggested or recommended by Jesus as a helpful experience to be sought?

8. Is the ministry always sensitive to the possible offense suffered by the unsaved in the audience who might be turned off by something that sometimes smacks of exhibitionism?

When you can answer all these questions to your own satisfaction, and then pray, "God, please be in charge here—be God in this and in all other experiences of my life, for Jesus' sake. Amen," then you can fall down all you want to.

PRINCIPLE: "Let all things be done decently and in order" (1 Corinthians 14:40).

13

Still More Failure

Are you ready now, after that digression, for a report on some further apparently unanswered prayers? Maybe after this final further input we can draw some conclusions about what God is up to in all these things. Let's give it a try.

One of the toughies involves a man you might remember from my first book, *How to Live Like a King's Kid*. His name was Ed, and he's the one who introduced me to the King of the Universe way back in 1954. You can imagine the kind of gratitude I've felt toward him since then.

You might even remember that one of the things that impressed me about Ed was that he was always smiling, in spite of his wife, but that's another story. Well, anyway, Ed got shed of wife number one, took on wife number two, shucked her, and moved to beautiful blue Hawaii and married wife number three. So much for his marital history.

You'll notice I'm not making comments about the wives, because I didn't know them that well. Whether Ed was right or wrong to break his ties doesn't matter at this point. The fact is, he did it.

One day I learned that Ed had cancer and was not expected to live. Naturally, we prayed for him in our prayer fellowship in Baltimore, and when I had a speaking engagement on the West Coast, the Lord impressed me to return home the long way, detouring twelve hundred miles by way of Hawaii so I could say *aloha* to Ed and lay hands on him and pray. Since Ed had introduced me to Jesus, I thought it was the least I could do. And surely God would honor my efforts.

Well, I went, met his wife and new baby son, laid hands on Ed, and prayed for him in the Spirit and with the under-standing, just as Paul would have done had he been there. I even talked with his Japanese surgeon, who explained to me that he had used the latest surgical techniques on Ed, split-ting him from goozle to gizzard, washing out all the cancer he couldn't cut out. He thought he got it all.

With the prayers of a righteous man added to the latest surgical techniques, we couldn't miss. Could we? Are you feeling as confident about the outcome as I was?

In spite of the confidence I felt, in six months, Ed was pushing up daisies—I mean, hibiscus.

Why?

Sin?

I dunno.

Bad diet?

I dunno.

Lack of faith on my part? I don't think so. I wouldn't have traveled twelve hundred miles to pray for a guy if I'd thought it wouldn't do any good, would I?

Lack of faith on Ed's part? Oh, Ed was such a great man of faith, God even used him to build faith in others. I re-member one time when he was visiting Robin, a little boy about five or six years old who had been born without a backbone and so had to live inside a corset contraption to hold him upright. The boy's parents weren't Christians, and Ed was working on the whole outfit in his prayers.

It had been a dry summer, and little Robin looked out the window and said, "Mr. Ed, if God is so real, and if He loves us so much, why doesn't He send us some rain? Look at the little birds—they're panting like my hound dog, they're so thirsty."

I suppose the Holy Spirit reminded Ed of the place in the Manufacturer's Handbook where God says, "... ye have not, because ye ask not" (James 4:2), so he decided to give Robin a little practice in being a doer of the Word.

"Well, Robin," Ed said, after reading him the Scripture, "I guess we haven't asked God for rain, have we? Why don't you ask Him right now and see what He'll do?"

Ed knew God would never disappoint a child, and Robin came as a little child, an action recommended by the Manufacturer's Handbook for folks young and old who are interested in enjoying the benefits of King's-kid living. Robin folded his hands, tucked them prayerfully under his little chin, squinched his eyes tight shut, and prayed, "Jesus, please send us some rain."

Then he looked out the window. There wasn't a cloud in sight.

"It didn't work," he said.

"Whoa, now," Ed said. "Don't you suppose it takes a little bit of time to make a cloud?" Then Ed read him James 1:4 and encouraged him to exercise a little patience. Robin agreed to give God half an hour to come up with some juicy clouds before he marked Him off.

Sometime during the half hour, when Robin looked out the window again, he saw a little cloud about the size of a man's hand. I guess it must have been something like the cloud God whomped up for Elijah back in 1 Kings 18:44. Like that cloud, it grew and grew until suddenly there was a humdinger of a gully washer, soaking everything within a five-block radius of Robin's house.

But the little boy never grew a backbone, even though Ed prayed for him many times. And Jesus didn't do anything about Ed's cancer, either, as far as we could tell.

Why not? I dunno. God's in charge here, and He could have had some purpose beyond the things I could see. That happens often. But sometimes He lets someone else in on His purpose, as was the case with my partner in Florida last year.

After speaking at an evening meeting at Christian Retreat in Bradenton, I went to the cafeteria for a second helping of one of my favorite desserts—Black Forest cake with a generous topping of ice cream. I knew it wasn't good for me, and I didn't need it. The Lord had long since made it clear to me that refined sugar was a no-no if I was interested in best results from the human mechanism, but—

Well, I don't need to explain these things to you. Most everybody knows how it is when you're about to succumb to a gloppy temptation. So I shoved God out of the way and let *me* be god, all the while pushing down the little "You'll be sorry" singsong I could hear down inside me. Then I sat down at a table with some of the brethren to enjoy the forbidden plateful.

An hour or so later, I got up from the table to go to my room and lie down, being acutely aware of an increasingly dizzy and light-headed sensation along with a tightness across my chest. After a few steps, everything went black, and I woke up on the floor. You never saw so much excitement! There was an ambulance, paramedics, a portable EKG machine, and much prayer. People laid on hands and prayed while I was prone. They even *sang* praises to God while they were waiting for the ambulance to arrive. I added a few squeaky falsettos of my own whenever I could save up enough breath.

Finally the attack was over, and the symptoms went away. Later, the Lord spoke loud and clear: *Hill, didn't I show you some time ago how refined sugar completely spoils the effects of any good foods you put in your system? Don't you remember I advised you to stop all intake of white sugar and white flour? Teacher, teachest thou not thyself?*

He was right, of course. I *knew* what I was supposed to do about those things, had even written my *How to Flip Your Flab—Forever,* incorporating those truths, but I had decided that evening that "just one little bite won't hurt," even though I knew better. Putting bad fuel into my system just about wiped me out in the bottomless pit of a sugar-low stupor. With my head spinning, and my emotions roller-coastering, my body chemistry simply disintegrated under an overdose of the Great American Drug. "But," you say, "if God made it, then why is it not good to eat?" God made *whole* sugar, which is nutritious. Man converted it into a drug through refining processes!

When I realized what had happened, I determined that if God allowed me to live through this experience, I would behave myself next time. Meanwhile, was all the emergency action necessary as a reminder to me to cool it in the sugar department, no matter how tempting the bait? Wasn't God overdoing things a bit, being a shade too dramatic?

As it turned out, He was doing something else far more important than putting me on notice. My partner, Liz, told me about the rest of it later. It seems there was an elderly gentleman, a newcomer to the camp, who was watching every move I made. He saw a preacher kneel, put his hands on my chest, and pray while I kept praising the Lord and singing as much as I was able. He was bug-eyed when I continued to praise the Lord while the paramedics were taking off my shirt and hooking me up to the EKG machine.

After all the confusion had died down, the old man shook his head and said, "I've heard that these people praise the Lord in difficult circumstances, but this is the first time I've ever seen them really put it to use in their own lives. It's made a believer out of me."

And so we both learned a lesson.

We never know who's watching, what one particular person God might be impressing with the reality of our walk with Him. It may be that's what this whole thing was about—that one elderly gentleman would come to a new level of faith. Suits me. When God's really in charge, anything can happen. He can bring good for others from our goofs and teach us a lesson at the same time.

Then there was another case with a highly unexpected outcome. Buck Freeman, my business partner for many years, had kept putting me off about surrendering to the Jesus I kept telling him about. "Lord, use every means possible to get his attention," I prayed. And one day Buck discovered he had a thoroughgoing case of cancer.

After his fourth operation, when he was declared to be incurable and dying, I was impressed to go to the hospital and pray for him. This time, he didn't put me on hold. He received the Lord, was released from the hospital, and came home. In a few weeks' time, he had gained forty pounds and was able to be outside walking around in his yard, apparently fit as a fiddle, witnessing to anybody who would listen. The doctors were calling it a miracle of remission from cancer. Buck even invited his doctor and me out to lunch one day, and we had a good time thanking Jesus for all He had done.

And then, all of a sudden, without any apparent reason, one day Buck died.

Why?

It is futility to try to explain why God lets such things happen. We get all tangled up when we try to figure out what God is doing in the life of a particular person. Sometimes, as we look at it, it seems that God has a single-faceted plan in the lives of some people. Maybe they have only a bit part to perform in the kingdom. Witnessing to his doctor and his neighbors could have been Buck's single-shot assignment. Mission fulfilled, at fourscore, he graduated.

We find quickie assignments in the lives of some Bible characters. Look at Philip and Matthias, mentioned one time and then never heard from again.

I recall reading about a symphony orchestra that imported a certain European musician to play a single passage in a whole symphony. When he had performed that to perfection, they sent him home. He had done what he was called to do. They didn't need him for anything else.

In our local fellowship was a medical doctor and his wife, both of them born again and filled with the Spirit, beautiful witnesses. Years ago, the woman came down with multiple sclerosis, a terrible disease that causes increasing paralysis and uncontrollable jerking muscle tremors. Naturally, she had the best medical treatment invented. But nothing helped. And no matter how many people prayed for her—and many did, because she and her husband were active in Full Gospel circles—she never showed any improvement. As far as anybody could pick up from being around her, God never did anything about her ailment except give her the grace to twitch in misery and torment and suffering and agony—praising the Lord the whole time, and never complaining.

Maybe that was her special assignment? If it was, how do you suppose God felt about the self-righteous, well-meaning folks who tried to make her feel guilty for not "receiving her healing"? I wouldn't want to trade places with them—or with her—would you?

"Someday I'll receive my complete healing," the woman used to tell us. I guess she has received it now. We buried her a few weeks ago.

Another woman of my acquaintance has Parkinson's disease. She's been prayed for and anointed with oil by everybody in the business. Instead of getting better, she's getting worse.

How come?

I dunno.

Eighteen years ago, singer Merrill Womach was flying his twin-engine plane when it crashed and exploded into flames. That he lived was a miracle. That he could sing better than ever was another. A miracle even happened to his face—but not the kind of miracle you might think. His face is still terribly scarred. But he's not bitter—he's thankful. And the joy shows through so much that he's actually pleasant to look at. What he has to say about it in *The Christian Reader* is so good I'd like to quote it:

> Across the country, especially on television, people are being told that if they have enough faith, God will heal them of anything. If they aren't healed, they are told they must have sin in their lives. That kind of statement is keeping more people depressed and discouraged than anything I know. I asked for healing, and others prayed for me for healing. I strongly believe God can miraculously transform my face into a baby's skin even now. But He doesn't. Yet I'm healed. God chose not to heal me physically, and that gives me an important entree when talking with others who have experienced accidents similar to mine.

The article goes on to say about Womach:

> There are few people better prepared to talk about trouble. He has survived without a hint of bitterness. He doesn't dwell on what might have been. Instead, he talks about the mercy of God that allowed him to survive and spread hope and joy to people through his songs and testimony.

When one suggests that he must have been born with lots of perseverance, Merrill insists, "I would be nothing but a pile of ashes in the Oregon forest without God's intervention. Every breath I take is given by him. And when I quote people my favorite Bible verse, 'I can do all things through Christ who strengthens me,' the emphasis is not on the 'I,' but on the 'Christ.' He's the reason I'm alive today."

Reprinted with permission from The Saturday Evening Post Company, © 1980.

Isn't that good? And take Joni, the young woman who seems so far to be scheduled to spend the rest of her life in a wheelchair. I've never met her, but I'm impressed that everywhere I turn, her attitude toward God is making her a source of huge comfort, according to 2 Corinthians 1, to many people who would hardly be able to listen to someone standing on his own two feet. What does she say about her situation? In an interview reported in the September 1980 *Bookstore Journal,* she says she read a book one day about the sovereignty of God that opened her eyes to a few things. But let her tell it:

> Until then I always thought my accident was an accident, that it was something the devil had schemed and God was helpless to prevent. [After she read the book, she was] convinced my accident was not an accident, but an injury which was part of His special plan for me. I also had the most overwhelming sense of comfort in the knowledge that God was in control. I realized my injury was not done capriciously, irresponsibly, or deliberately, but was done with a motive, a reason, and with a purpose. . . . To know that God held the reasons in His hands was enough for me.

So often these days, I have to confess out loud that I don't know why God does things the way He does. I used to try to find reasons, because I was trying to protect God's reputation for goodness. My explanations generally exonerated God at the expense of the sick persons, accusing them of having insufficient faith, hidden sin, impatience, unteachable spirits, unforgiveness, or hanging some other kind of guilt trip on them. No wonder they didn't get out of their wheelchairs when I prayed for them. They might have gone away sicker than when they came, because of the condemnation that was an unconscious, intrinsic part of my prayers for their healing.

Now I see that the explanation was never so simple as I tried to make it. I wish I *could* come up with a nice, ready answer like I used to, all documented and dogmatized. But today I have to admit I don't know why He heals somebody on the spot and seems to totally ignore someone else who might seem even more worthy of His attention. I just don't know. And when the agony drags on for years and years, I still don't know. But I've begun to believe He has a reason—a *good* reason.

What freedom there is in being able to say that, and not having to condemn folks for resentment, unbelief, impatience, an unteachable spirit, or any of the rest of the "roadblock" reasons. I don't even have to lay a guilt trip on you for putting bad fuel in your human mechanism, because I've known people who were even sicker whom God healed without requiring any alteration in their menu department. Although this universe is *mostly* a matter of cause and effect, there's something else involved, too, that intangible factor related to God's purpose in it all. It's unprogrammable, and we won't be able to figure it out if we ponder it for a thousand years.

Somehow I've come to a point in my life where that's not a frustration to me. Can you believe it? I guess you could say that at last I'm satisfied that I can trust Him, no matter what. I'm actually glad He's in charge here.

PRINCIPLE: "Therefore, since we are surrounded by such a great cloud of witnesses, let us throw off everything that hinders and the sin that so easily entangles, and let us run with perseverance the race marked out for us. Let us fix our eyes on Jesus, the author and perfecter of our faith, who for the joy set before him endured the cross, scorning its shame, and sat down at the right hand of the throne of God. Consider him who endured such opposition from sinful men, so that you will not grow weary and lose heart" (Hebrews 12:1–3 NIV).

14

Parenthesis # 2

I'm ready for another parenthesis, aren't you? I mean, all those folks dying and getting burned and winding up in wheelchairs can get to you after a while. For a *big* antidote, you can go read some of my other books that report victories almost exclusively instead of cases where the action went the other way. But if you don't happen to have some of them handy, try this chapter for size. Maybe it'll cheer you up to where you'll be looking down at wormholes instead of up at 'em.

The report concerns the experience of an orthodontist friend of mine who could have learned more about the dentition of lions than he wanted to know. It happened on the Serengeti Plain of Tanzania in 1977.

The orthodontist—Bagley's his name—and a friend were camping in a game park in Africa—no guns allowed. One day Bagley read a book called *Maneaters of Tsavo,* probably not the best choice of reading material for peace of mind in an area where you could find out how it felt to be a man eaten.

The next night, he was rudely awakened by his companion, a guy named Don.

"Quiet!" Don whispered, shaking him awake and then explaining that Bagley had been snoring so loudly that a lion had answered him with a roar. While Bagley tried not to breathe, the lion's roar came again, from about twenty feet outside the tent, which vibrated at the intensity of the sound.

Bagley didn't feel comfortable, having read the scary book. There was another reason, too. Two days before, in that same area, a woman had been dragged out of her tent by a lion when she had screamed at him. Bagley and Don decided not to scream.

But what do you do when a marauding lion is outside your tent and your car is too far away to allow you to run for it and get there still inside your skin? Pray? They did. "Lord, please save me."

The lion kept roaring, drawing closer and closer. What next? It entered Bagley's head to praise the Lord, along the lines recommended by the Manufacturer's Handbook where it says, "In every thing give thanks: for this is the will of God in Christ Jesus concerning you" (1 Thessalonians 5:18). Bagley began, having nothing to lose.

"Lord, thank You for the lion. Thank You for no gun. Thank You that the car's too far away to save us. Thank You for being here with us."

The more the lion roared, the more Bagley found for which to praise and thank the Lord. He'd never before realized how much he had for which he could be thankful—friends, family, situations, attitudes, opportunities, and most of all Jesus, of course.

He didn't know how it was going to turn out, but he was thankful to know he was in the will of God. It's always good to know that. And somehow, the longer he praised the Lord, the less afraid he was of the lion. Praise really drove the fear away.

When dawn finally came, the lion vanished. As the men broke camp, they discovered claw marks and rips in the canvas about a foot from where Bagley's head had been!

That means the lion had been trying to get to them before either of the men ever woke up!

Driving across the plain that day, seeing more wild animals than he could count, Bagley knew he had learned something about praise. He had learned something else, too: "... before they call, I will answer," was the way the Bible put it in Isaiah 65:24.

Rejoicing about these things, Bagley was impressed to open his Bible for a special Word from the Lord. The verse that caught his eye? Daniel 6:22, what else? "My God hath sent his angel, and hath shut the lions' mouths, that they have not hurt me...."

Isn't that a faith builder, though? Thanks, Bagley, for giving me a chance to share it with the brethren.

Now, back to business.

15

Why Are We Here?

What are You up to, God? What's it all about? What do You want with us? Who are we, anyhow, and why are we here? What is Your purpose for us?

Several years ago, a comic-strip character asked God the Psalmist's question: "What is man, that thou art mindful of him?" (Psalms 8:4). The strip showed that the little guy was expecting a lofty answer giving some noble reason for man's existence on Planet Earth. What he got, through the pen and ink of the cartoonist, has to be the greatest put-down of the century:

> The weeds
> need
> the carbon dioxide.

Since there are plenty of people in places where the weeds have all given way to concrete parking lots and chewing-gum-studded sidewalks, that can't be the whole answer. Let's look a little further.

The Catholic kids in Baltimore used to walk around memorizing the contents of a little book called a "penny catechism." It's probably up to a buck fifty by now. The best I can remember, the catechism had a statement of God's purpose for man that went something like this: "to know God, to love God, and to fellowship with Him forever."

That sounds pretty good—biblical, too. Not too far from what God said through Micah when he wrote, "What does the Lord require of you? To act justly and to love mercy and to walk humbly with your God" (Micah 6:8 NIV).

Exploring the Manufacturer's Handbook for God's answer to the question, I found a number of Scriptures on the subject. They didn't all dovetail together exactly, which is fortunate. If they had, I'd have been tempted to compress them into a nice, neat, theological package, tie it with a string, and sell it to the highest bidder, who would become *the* authority who could parrot the "right" answer whenever "they" asked the question. As it is, all I can present are some separately packaged, scripturally based observations that you can hang together any way you choose. What you do with them is your business, not mine.

In the beginning, in Genesis, it sounded as though God made man to rule over the creatures of the earth (1:26), to bear fruit and multiply (1:28), to take care of the Garden of Eden (2:15), and to keep from eating from the tree of knowledge of good and evil (2:17). The last part, which sounded the easiest, was the one that proved impossible to him.

Interesting, isn't it, that Adam couldn't *multiply* until God had performed some mathematical operations of His own. In history's first recorded operation of any sort, mathematical or otherwise, He *subtracted* a rib from Adam's side in order to *add* a helpmate and *divide* the chores. I'd never realized that before. Amazing what a fellow can learn with a little digging into the Word.

This example seems to say that in this instance, at least, when God told man to do one thing, He did three times as much Himself to make Adam's part possible.

Hmmm. Interesting. I've experienced that kind of help,

too. The Manufacturer's Handbook says that He gives us everything we need for life and godliness (1 Peter 1:3). Godliness would certainly include obedience to what He requires, wouldn't it?

Now, where were we? Oh, yes. Back to Adam.

Adam's assignments didn't sound bad to start with, but as everybody knows, he soon sold out to Slue Foot. The fruit of that no-no tree was just too great a temptation to pass up, especially when Adam's wife offered him a bite. The result was that Adam got a transfer. He was reassigned to do his gardening in a wider territory—outside Eden—and there began to be plenty of thorns and thistles to plague him.

But the Manufacturer's Handbook goes on to indicate that after Adam's fall, there was more to God's purpose for man than being a daddy, a farmer, and a zoo keeper. Let's look at some of the Scriptures that tell about our new role.

One important facet of our purpose as residents on this spacecraft called Planet Earth is plainly expressed in the Gospel of John: "You did not choose me, but I chose you to go and bear fruit—fruit that will last," Jesus said (John 15:16 NIV). What is the fruit of a Christian? Baby Christians, of course. Our heavenly objective here is heavenly obstetrics, and living in such a way that others will want what we've got, and then we can deliver it to them. In other words, we can help them to get born again, into a right relationship with God, and they can become fruit bearers along with us.

In connection with our fruit-bearing purpose, I found Jesus making one of the great prayer promises. *If* we bear fruit, "*Then* the Father will give you whatever you ask in my name" (John 15:16 NIV, my italics), Jesus said. Sounds to me as though He's promising to provide whatever we need for fruit bearing; how does it sound to you? If we ask for something we don't need for fruit bearing, but to "spend what you get on your pleasures" (James 4:3 NEB), our motives are out of order, James tells us. Then, at best, the results are iffy.

Jesus expressed our assignment in the Gospel of Matthew in words that we call "the Great Commission": "Go then and make disciples of all the nations, baptize them into the name of the Father, the Son, and the Holy Spirit, and teach them to *practice* all the commands that I have given you" (Matthew 18:19, 20 WILLIAMS).

That little word *practice* in the last part of verse 20 makes you sit up and take notice, doesn't it. Reading from a variety of translations can open your eyes to things you hadn't realized before.

Re-reading the letters of the New Testament to see what they had to say about man's purpose, I was impressed with the facts stated over and over again that we are created to be a holy people, a people set apart for God, doing works for Him, glorifying Him, praising Him, being His mouthpiece, His holy temple, becoming His children, being conformed not to the world, but to Jesus, growing up to be mature saints who can rule and reign with Him for the rest of eternity....

Here's how some of the writers expressed these things: "... called according to His purpose ... to be conformed to the likeness of his son ..." (Romans 8:28, 29 NIV).

"For he chose us in him before the creation of the world to be holy and blameless in his sight. In love he predestined us to be adopted as his sons through Jesus Christ ..." (Ephesians 1:4, 5 NIV).

"We have been destined and appointed to live for the praise of His glory" (Ephesians1:12 AMPLIFIED).

"[God] has saved us and called us to a holy life ... because of his own purpose and grace" (2 Timothy 1:9 NIV).

"For we are God's workmanship, created in Christ Jesus

to do good works, which God prepared in advance for us to do" (Ephesians 2:10 NIV).

"The Spirit himself testifies with our spirit that we are God's children. Now if we are children, then we are heirs— heirs of God and co-heirs with Christ . . . " (Romans 8:16, 17 NIV).

"Your body, you know, is the temple of the Holy Spirit . . ." (1 Corinthians 6:19 JERUSALEM).

How does that last one work? Peter explained it this way: "So come to Him, our living Stone—the stone rejected by men but choice and precious in the sight of God. Come, and let yourselves be built as living stones, into a spiritual temple . . ." (1 Peter 2:4, 5 NEB).

Then Peter went on to sum it all up, in a grand symphonic crescendo: "But you are the chosen race, the King's priests, the holy nation, God's own people, chosen to proclaim the wonderful acts of God, who called you out of darkness into his own marvelous light" (1 Peter 2:9 TEV).

Chosen to proclaim the wonderful acts of God! That's something, isn't it! A long way from providing the weeds with carbon dioxide.

These are clearly high and holy purposes for all of us in the here and now, and there are other Scriptures that speak just as plainly of the glories that are to come. But in the midst of all this good news, there are many other verses that sound grim and a little bit scary. Do you have the courage to look at them with me?

For openers, look at what Jesus said in John 16:33: ". . . In this world you will have trouble" (NIV). In the same Gospel, He promised that we would have persecution (John 15:20).

And in Acts?

When they had preached the Gospel to that town and made disciples of many of the people, they went back to

Lystra and Iconium and Antioch, Establishing and
strengthening the souls and the hearts of the disciples,
urging and warning and encouraging them to stand firm
in the faith, and telling them that it is through many
hardships and tribulations we must enter the kingdom of
God.

Acts 14:21, 22 AMPLIFIED

Peter echoed all that when he said, ". . . now for a little
while you may have had to suffer grief in all kinds of trials"
(1 Peter 1:6 NIV).

What kinds of trials was Peter talking about? I got a clue
from Hebrews 11 where I saw what the Old Testament
heroes of the faith had to contend with. Just listen:
". . . others were tortured . . . others had trial of cruel mock-
ings and scourgings, yea, moreover of bonds and imprison-
ment: They were stoned, they were sawn asunder, were
tempted, were slain with the sword . . . destitute, afflicted,
tormented" (verses 35–37).

Back then, apparently faith in God didn't guarantee a
comfortable, plush living on Planet Earth, did it. And I understand from other sources that Jesus' disciples exited this
stage of eternal life as martyrs via such exclusive, unenvi-
able, one-to-a-customer-please methods as hanging, decapi-
tation, and by special request, crucifixion in an upside-down
position.

I'm not exactly interested in standing in line to follow in
their footsteps, are you? I wonder where we ever got the idea
that King's-kid living on Planet Earth was supposed to be
all Cadillacs and crepes suzette?

Maybe the whole point is that what is in store for us hereafter is so wonderful that we can afford to start rejoicing
now for everything, even the raunchy things we might have
to endure in order to be made fit for heaven. Paul seemed to
think that was the case. Do you remember what he said

about it? Here it is: "In my opinion whatever we may have to go through now ["our present sufferings" NIV] is less than nothing compared with the magnificent future God has in store for us" (Romans 8:18 PHILLIPS). The heading of the paragraph in which that verse appears in the Phillips translation is "Present distress is temporary and negligible." I say, "Right on, Brother Paul! Right on, Brother Phillips!"

We can put up with anything we have to, knowing there will be an end to it and a beginning to glorious things.

Possibly James had a similar thought in mind when he wrote that we could "Consider it pure joy . . . whenever you face trials of many kinds, because you know that the testing of your faith develops perseverance. Perseverance must finish its work so that you may be mature and complete, not lacking anything" (James 1:2–4 NIV).

Mature and complete, not lacking anything? My guess is that God doesn't want any half-baked King's kids, so He does what He has to do to grow us up. Here's Paul's comment about all this: "I am quite certain that the One who began this good work in you will see that it is finished when the Day of Christ Jesus comes" (Philippians 1:6 JERUSA-LEM). I expect that will be the day when we'll "be like him, because we shall see him as he ["really" TEV] is" (1 John 3:2 NEB).

To me, that's a sight worth holding on for. Is it to you?

What Paul wrote to Timothy is something else that makes me want to hang on to the end: "If we endure, we will also reign with Him . . ." (2 Timothy 2:12 NIV).

Let's see. Before we got sidetracked looking at the troubles we are promised this side of gloryland, we were talking about our purpose for existence as it's revealed in the pages of the Manufacturer's Handbook, weren't we.

In addition to the general purposes we all have, there are some special individualized purposes for each one of us, too.

I heard about some of them this morning as I was driving along, listening to some New Testament Bible tapes. Like you, I don't always have the time to do all the Bible reading I need in order to stay in top form physically, emotionally, and spiritually, so I do the next best thing and listen to someone else read the Word when I have to keep my eyes glued to the highway. (Send a stamped, self-addressed envelope to the address at the end of chapter 1, and I'll send you details about how you can get an album of my favorite Bible tapes so you can keep packing the Word of God down in your gizzard practically twenty-four hours a day.)

Listening this morning, I heard Paul say that God's purpose was for us King's kids to be gardeners of one kind or another, in order that at harvest time, there would be a crop of souls. Had you ever noticed that? It's right there near the front end of First Corinthians: ". . . the Lord has assigned to each his task. I planted the seed, Apollos watered it . . ." (3:5, 6). And in the same letter, in the twelfth chapter, I heard that all of us King's kids—"living stones," Peter called us (1 Peter 2:5)—are designed to fit into the Body of Christ. Here's how that went:

> Now here is what I am trying to say: All of you together are the one body of Christ and each one of you is a separate and necessary part of it. Here is a list of some of the parts he has placed in his church, which is his body: Apostles, Prophets—those who preach God's Word, Teachers, Those who do miracles, Those who have the gift of healing; Those who can help others, Those who can get others to work together, Those who speak in languages they have never learned.
>
> 1 Corinthians 12:27, 28 TLB

God had already told them about the gifts of the Spirit, the special equipment each one of us would need for carrying out our specific assignment as fruit bearers for Him, because He didn't want us to be ignorant of these things (1 Corinthians 12:1–11). (I have explained all the gifts of the Spirit in detail in *How to Live in High Victory* and in my *Gifts of the Holy Spirit* album, so I won't go into all that here.) Peter said we were to use any gift we had received "to serve others, faithfully administering God's grace in its various forms" (1 Peter 4:10 NIV).

Have you ever noticed how difficult it is to stick to one subject when you start looking up some topic in the Bible? All the words are so full of life, there's just no good stopping place. One thing leads to another, and then to another. But let's make ourselves get back closer to the topic we've been pursuing here: our general and specific assignments on Planet Earth.

Living as God's children in whatever role He equips us to fulfill, we are His fruit bearers and ministers of life in specific, tailor-made, just-for-us assignments.

Paul said he was chosen to be the apostle to the Gentiles. Esther was "born for such a time as this" to rescue her people. Moses was chosen to lead the Israelites out of Egypt. Philip was chosen to go down to the Gaza Road and harvest the Ethiopian eunuch for the Lord. Lazarus was chosen to be raised from the dead. Eutychus was chosen to fall asleep under Paul's long-winded sermon, accidentally fall off the windowsill, and be raised from the dead when he was picked up off the ground.

God's special assignments weren't limited to the "good guys"; He even had a special assignment for Pharaoh. In his letter to the Romans, Paul reported that God had said to Pharaoh, "I raised you up for this very purpose, that I might display my power in you and that my name might be proclaimed in all the earth" (Romans 9:17 NIV).

Pharaoh, like Judas, had a tough assignment, didn't he. I

wouldn't have wanted to be in his shoes. But it looks to me, according to the Manufacturer's Handbook, as though he didn't have much say-so about it. God was in charge of dishing out the good and the bad.

"But that's not fair!" someone's bound to howl.

Whoa! You're out of line again. Who's to say what's fair or not fair? If God's in charge, He's the One making the rules, right? That principle is echoed over and over again in His rule book. Want to consider a couple of for-instances?

Look at the ninth chapter of Romans. There Paul reports what God said to Rebecca when she was expecting Jacob and Esau

> before her twin children were born and before either had done good or evil. In order to stress that God's choice is free, since it depends on the one who calls, not on human merit, Rebecca was told: *The elder shall serve the younger,* or as scripture says elsewhere: *I showed my love for Jacob and my hatred for Esau.*
>
> Romans 9:11–13 JERUSALEM

God must have known you would protest about His apparently "unfair" treatment of Esau, because Paul went on to write, "What then shall we say? Is God unjust? Not at all! For He says to Moses, 'I will have mercy on whom I have mercy, and I will have compassion on whom I have compassion.' . . . Therefore God has mercy on whom he wants to have mercy, and he hardens whom he wants to harden" (Romans 9:14, 15, 18 NIV).

In case you're still sputtering at the injustice of it all, God knew that would happen, too, and He has a further Word for sputterers:

> One of you will say to me: "Then why does God still blame us? For who resists his will?" But who are you, O

man, to talk back to God? "Shall what is formed say to
him who formed it, 'Why did you make me like this?'
Does not the potter have the right to make out of the same
lump of clay some pottery for noble purposes and some
for common use?"

Romans 9:19–21 NIV

It sounds to me as though God is in charge of all these
things—whether we like it or not. How does it sound to you?

"Oh, but God doesn't do 'bad things'!" someone is still
chirping in the background. Consult your insurance policy.
Doesn't it blame God for a lot of disastrous things under the
heading "acts of God"? But don't take the underwriter's
word for it. Don't take anyone else's word for it. Look at
what God says, right there in black and white:

"I form the light and create darkness, I bring prosperity
and create disaster; I, the Lord, do all these things" (Isaiah
45:7 NIV).

Did that verse blow all your fuses, or are you still with
me? Amazing, isn't it, that God would say He creates disaster. We wouldn't expect Him to do that. And that Isaiah
Scripture isn't an isolated, one-of-a-kind that we can dismiss
as a typographical error. Look at Amos 3:6: "When disaster
comes to a city, has not the Lord caused it?" (NIV).

There are a number of other verses that suggest that
God's ways of looking at things are not the same as ours,
and that some of His purposes for a particular person might
not sound praiseworthy to us in our limited, finite way of
looking at things.

A mother of a young child gave me an analogy one day
explaining the way these things looked to her. She said that
our view and judgment of things is like that of a hypotheti-
cal visitor from outer space who knew nothing of our ways
of doing business here on Planet Earth. The visitor—visual-
ize him as a little green man with pointed ears, if you like—

peeked through the keyhole of the door into a doctor's examining room. There, what he saw through his keyhole vision looked terrible! A loving (!?) mother was holding down a squealing, screaming, squirming kid so the smiling nurse could poke a mile-long needle into the padded portion of the kid's posterior.

There's no way a little green man lacking inside information could conclude that was a good and loving thing for the mama to do. But the torment connected with the administration of the immunization shot was pure joy for the mother compared to the contemplation of seeing her darling dying from "hydripthia" or whatever the current malady was that was wiping out people who had not been immunized.

"Our view of what God is doing is sometimes as limited as that of the little green man," the mother told me.

"But Brother Hill!" someone's shrieking, and I can tell from the tone of the shriek that I have a label maker in the audience. "Do you mean to tell me that you're saying that the end justifies the means?"

Glad you asked that. Nope, that's not what I'm saying at all. I'm not making doctrines or hanging labels on this trip, I told you. Too much danger of computer programming God if I fall for that exalting of my intellect. All I'm saying is what I've said. Somebody with a keyhole-limited view, ignorant of mama's purposes on well-baby checkup day at the clinic, could leap to wrong conclusions about mama's goodness. And our view of what God's up to is infinitely more restricted than that.

Speaking the truth in love, then, as it's recommended so we will all grow up (Ephesians 4:15), I want to lay down a new rule: "Don't hang labels. Don't call names." God's in charge here. He often cuts off the trickle of goodies to turn on the full stream of His abundance. And most times, what we consider good stands in the way of His best. That's why, when we're grateful for what we have, we're ready for something better. Otherwise, our negative attitudes and grumbling would carry over into the next blessing and spoil that one, too.

What's the antidote for all our fears and uncertainties about what God is up to? "Rejoice evermore. Pray without ceasing. In every thing give thanks: for this is the will of God in Christ Jesus concerning you" (1 Thessalonians 5:16–18).

This simple act of practicing "all the commands I have given you" opens the door for God to arrange the results.

Don't make doctrines about God that God hasn't made for Himself. Just explore the Word, and let its many-faceted fullness get inside you and give you light. When the Psalmist wrote, "The entrance of your words gives light . . ." (Psalms 119:130 NIV), he was probably talking about all of them. In the same Psalm, he had said, "I know, O Lord, that your laws are righteous, and in faithfulness you have afflicted me" (Psalms 119:75 NIV).

Why does God do all the things He does? Because He loves us, that's why. That's not a doctrine I have made up; it's a truth that permeates His Word. Sometimes what He does, doesn't look like love, but we're keyhole peepers, remember, and God chastens those He loves (Hebrews 12:6). None of us enjoys chastening or punishment, but it's necessary for our good. "Later on, however, it produces a harvest of righteousness and peace for those who have been trained by it" (Hebrews 12:11 NIV). The shot may hurt—but afterward, we'll be glad we had it.

In the same chapter of Isaiah where God tells us He is the One who creates disaster, He has this to say about His purposes in everything He does: "So that from the rising of the sun to the place of its setting men may know there is none besides me. I am the Lord, and there is no other" (Isaiah

45:6 NIV). It's the same thing He says in the New Testament through Paul. After he explained that we become brand-new creatures when we are in Christ (2 Corinthians 5:17), Paul wrote of God's purposes—for Himself and for us—in these words:

> It is all God's work. It was God who reconciled us to himself through Christ and gave us the work of handing on this reconciliation. In other words, God in Christ was reconciling the world to himself, not holding men's faults against them, and he has entrusted to us the news that they are reconciled. So we are ambassadors for Christ; it is as though God were appealing through us, and the appeal that we make in Christ's name is: be reconciled to God. For our sake God made the sinless one into sin, so that in him we might become the goodness of God.
>
> 2 Corinthians 5:18–21 JERUSALEM

Do I hear a hallelujah out there anywhere? Whatever it takes to get me where God wants me, here I am, Lord. You're in charge. And that's just fine with me, whether I understand it all or not.

If the Scriptures we have just examined are an accurate reflection of God's purposes for us, then I could wreck the whole program by going through the hospitals and wiping out all illness, couldn't I? I mean, in my sojourn here on Planet Earth, I have seen many people come to the Lord through the desperation of a hospital trip. You've probably observed the same thing, if you've lived long enough.

Why, if all my prayers for healing were answered on the spot, I could actually send folks away rejoicing in perfect health, only to find themselves later headed down the tube on the wrong end of a fire shovel. Often people suffer and find God in the midst of their suffering, the very God they rejected when they were hale and hearty and thought they didn't need Him. Remember my friend Buck Freeman, for instance. And in my own case, every drink brought me closer to the day of desperation when I would cry out, "God, help me!"

There's no particular point in keeping a corpse alive unless you're going to get him saved somewhere along the line. To give the starving millions bread without any plans for giving them the Gospel may look like compassion, but it's just giving them full bellies instead of empty ones and so merely postponing their trip to hell.

Is it ever God's will for a man to be a drunk? If it's the only way He can get saved, maybe it is. Alcoholism just happened to be my ticket to heaven. Some other kind of sickness might be someone else's ticket there.

When we consider that God is sovereign God, and that maybe His long-range plans for His people are better than our short-range ones, His answering our prayers specifically, exactly as we pray them, could be second best in some cases. But when we pray in the Spirit, we can count on the Holy Spirit to search our hearts and our real needs and come up with an answer suited to our needs instead of to our wants. When we forget the past and press on to the mark of the high calling of God in Christ Jesus (Philippians 3:14) by doing the next thing, knowing that all things really do work together for good—God's and ours—then we are living as if we really believe "God's in charge here."

This brings us full circle, in a way, back to our original and all-pervading purpose of multiplying the ranks of King's kids on Planet Earth, beginning with us. It's a good place to stop this chapter, where we've looked at what God wants us to do, and start on the next—how to do it.

Are you ready?

PRINCIPLE: "But you are the chosen race, the King's priests, the holy nation, God's own people, chosen to proclaim the wonderful acts of God, who called you out of the darkness into his own marvelous light" (1 Peter 2:9 TEV).

PS: Have you been breathing as you've plowed through this chapter? Then you've been providing the weeds with carbon dioxide, like it or not. You've been helping the thistles and thorns to grow. But you've helped the flowers and trees, too. Does that help you understand anything about the nature of God's mercy in the midst of His being in charge of everything? It does me.

"He causes his sun to rise on the evil and the good, and sends rain on the righteous and the unrighteous" (Matthew 5:45 NIV). It's something to think about.

16

How *Not* to Do It

From the title of this chapter, you can see that I've changed my mind. Instead of looking first at how to go about cooperating with God for the fulfillment of His purpose for us, I'm going to begin with a few observations about how *not* to do it. With those negatives cleared away, we'll be all set to go full speed ahead in a positive direction, letting God be God, fully in charge of everything, with no hindering "help" from the well-meaning schemes of men.

Ready, set, let's go!

And let's begin by looking at some of the mistakes we make that have a tendency to try to keep God from being God in particular circumstances. Most of them are somehow related to the human habit we've been trying to break throughout these pages—that of inventing man-made doctrines about everything.

For years I have been teaching about the removal of roadblocks that prevent heaven's best in the lives of King's kids. (You can read up on them in *How to Live Like a King's Kid* and *How to Live in High Victory*.) But once we confess our helplessness in ridding ourselves of them—impatience, unforgiveness, resentment, unbelief, gossiping, complaining, an unteachable spirit, and all the rest of the ugly parade—and look to Jesus in each situation to handle them, we have to acknowledge that there is still something going on that doesn't fit doctrines based on our overall premise that King's kids can have the best of everything in the here and now as well as in the hereafter. Some of the things we observe just don't seem to fit into God's overall scheme of things.

We used to dismiss such situations by laying a guilt trip on the person who refused to be healed, accusing him of hidden sin, weak faith, unforgiveness, or some other fault. But something tells me that now it's time to explore another more likely and far more charitable explanation for the failure of our prayers in some situations.

Let's look at a big reason for God's variations on a theme. As Paul put it, we need to come to an understanding of what the will of the Lord is (Ephesians 5:17).

As I have looked at these things over a period of time, I have come to the conclusion that the problem is that we've made doctrines that God simply doesn't choose to follow. Take a for-instance:

We've read the valid principle, stated in the Scripture, "He [Jesus] healed them all" (Matthew 12:15). We've read another valid principle which states, "God is no respecter of persons" (Acts 10:34), and checked it out in several different translations to make sure we had a handle on what it means: "God shows no partiality" (RSV); "God treats everyone on the same basis" (TEV); "God does not show favoritism" (NIV). Satisfied the words meant what we thought they meant, we've lifted them out of context (Peter was talking here about the fact that salvation was for every nationality, but we've neatly ignored that) and glued these two Scriptures together with a few others to whomp up an "infallible doctrine package" that says, "God always heals everybody of everything right now if they confess it. What you say is what you get—unless there is hidden sin in your life."

What a killer!

When the observable facts refuse to fit our doctrine, we go howling off to God, complaining that He broke His own rules, when in fact, He hasn't broken anything. (I wonder sometimes why He doesn't break all our necks, don't you, for presuming to tell Him what to do?) Anyhow, He is, as usual, true to Himself and not to our man-made doctrines about Him and how He will act. God is not programmable. We can't punch Him into a computer and say how He will always act. He does *new* things whenever He takes a notion. Who's to say He can't do exactly as He pleases?

It is simply impossible to build doctrines that will cover every individual in every case without ending in total confusion. God's the only one who knows what He's out to accomplish in a particular life and the means He has chosen to use to accomplish that purpose. God isn't someone we can put in a box. He's infinitely more complicated and multidimensional than any doctrine we could ever figure out. Remember what we observed about how He healed the blind as the cases are reported in the Gospels—some with mud, some without mud, some on the installment plan. . . .

It's hard to make a foolproof doctrine out of that, because God might choose to do it a different way next time. I suspect He doesn't want us to try harder to figure Him out, but to let Him be God any way He chooses in circumstances where men have imperfect vision. "Who has known the mind of the Lord?" (Romans 11:34 NIV). The only answer is, "No one, Lord. Please pardon our presumption."

Although there is no variableness in God (James 1:17), He is a God of infinite variety. He hasn't run out of unique designs for quickly melting snowflakes, much less for humans who will live forever.

A bottom line here, as I see it, is that when men keep making doctrines in an attempt to insure success, they are almost guaranteed to insure just the opposite. (But don't make a doctrine out of that!)

"What you say is what you get!" is one of the most widespread doctrines in the Charismatic movement. It's easy to see how it sprang up. When we look at Jesus and realize He never failed but *always* got what He said—for Himself and for other people—we have a natural tendency to think it will be that simple for us. As a result, we have gone around spouting the formula without doing any research into the background, thereby missing the whole key to every situation.

For Jesus, saying and getting were the same thing, because he didn't say anything except what His Father commanded Him to say (John 12:49, 50). In other words, He was always absolutely sure of His Father's will before He opened His mouth. That's why He could stand there outside Lazarus' tomb and thank the Father that the Father always heard Him. First, He heard the Father. Our doctrine didn't take into account the fact that we don't always do that.

Once man had made a false doctrine labeled "What you say is what you get," or "According to your faith be it unto you," he had a tendency to use it to condemn others. If it didn't work that way for them, he'd point an accusing finger and bellow, "Bad confession, brother!" or "Where's your faith?" Even when he didn't say these things out loud, the person in need picked up the condemnation from his body English that probably also shrieked, "You dirty old sinner, you!"

Yes—I'm answering some nitpickers in the shadows— Jesus *did* say, "According to your faith be it unto you" (Matthew 9:29), but at other times He didn't mention faith at all. He didn't say Lazarus had any faith—but He called him out of the tomb anyhow. He didn't say that the man let down through the roof on a stretcher had any faith. In that case, He looked at the faith of the four friends, the roof wreckers, and told the man sick with the palsy that his sins were forgiven and he could take up his bed and go home. And He didn't say anything about the faith of the Gadarene demoniac, and apparently there were no four friends to help him out with their faith, but Jesus treated him perfectly anyway.

The point is, and let me repeat it, Almighty God is just plain too complicated for our simple one-dimensional doctrines about anything. In the New Testament, God is deliberately unique in His actions in every situation, with every action tailored to a particular event. There are no generalities that can cover them all. Even Heinz with his fifty-seven varieties can't hold a candle to God. We'd be in an awful pickle if he could.

"Jesus always healed them all, and by His stripes we *are* healed!" is a doctrine based on Bible truth but one which overlooks individual circumstances which often determine results. The bottom line is, some are *not* healed, *ever*, in this lifetime!

Thus, in His hometown, Jesus could not do any miracles, except lay His hands on a *few* sick people and heal them (Mark 6:5). And think about the cripple who lay at the Gate Beautiful begging for all those years. Why didn't Jesus heal him when He passed by instead of saving his case for Peter and John to handle? (Acts 3:1–16).

That's enough for a start. I'll let you explore the rest of the Scriptures for yourself to see how many cases you find where the facts don't fit into the doctrines you've heard or invented. When you've finished, don't be disappointed; don't think you have to come to God's defense, but join me in a happy hallelujah that God's in charge here, doing what He chooses to do, to accomplish His purposes for His children.

Another deadly doctrine we need to look at deals with the matter of how many times we're supposed to pray for a particular thing before we put it on the shelf. Some doctrines have been made from Mark 11:24. The infallible Scripture goes like this: "Whatever you ask for in prayer, believe that you have received it, and it will be yours" (NIV).

Everything Jesus said about prayer is true, because Jesus is the truth. But this one Scripture is not *all* He ever said about prayer. Still, some folks have taken this verse, looked at the verb tenses, and gotten all excited, winding up with a doctrine that says, "If you pray for a thing more than once, that proves you think you didn't receive it the first time you prayed; therefore you were praying with unbelief—so, from now on, don't ever pray more than once."

Poor things! Just think of the blessings they might have missed! Apparently, to jolt these doctrines, Jesus prayed twice for one eye patient, with 100 percent success. And I remember Paul prayed three times about something and didn't get it. Further, I heard a tape on which one of the great faith teachers confessed 539 times that he was healed before anything visible happened. On the 540th time, his healing was manifested. But don't make a doctrine out of these things. Three isn't a magic negative number, and 540 isn't a magic positive number. It's just that God does what He pleases.

In the case of our prayers for the sick, I've observed that sometimes we see results, sometimes we don't. If we quit praying at the first flush of failure, our only testimony may be, "It didn't work." But if we keep on applying the power of prayer, we may be rewarded with real victory that people can see.

A Catholic priest named McNutt has come up with a concept that he calls "soaking prayer," where prayer and prayer and still more prayer is applied with rather remarkable results in some cases. We don't know why this works, but it seems to be very beneficial. Maybe it's the result of a transfer of energy from one system to another—from heaven to earth, as we magnify His name by asking Him to do something for us.

It's not that the last prayer finally gets results, but it's the cumulative effect of *all* the prayers that brings fruit in the form of the very thing we need.

We sometimes see the same dramatic effect where a number of people decide to fast and pray together for a certain intention for a shorter period of time. In this case, I guess you might call it "flooding prayer" instead of "soaking prayer," but the result in either case seems sometimes to be an inundation that heaven cannot resist.

Is "soaking prayer" scriptural? Of course! Matthew 7:7, 8 says it loud and clear: "Keep on asking and it will be given you. . . . For every one who keeps on asking receives" (AM-PLIFIED).

The folks who invented the "pray once and quit" doctrine didn't have the whole story. Doctrine makers never do.

Let's wind this chapter up with the warning Jesus quoted to the Pharisees from the Prophet Isaiah: "These people honor me with their lips, but their hearts are far from Me. They worship me in vain; their teachings are but rules taught by men" (Matthew 15:8, 9 NIV).

PRINCIPLE: "Do not add to what I command you and do not subtract from it, but keep the commands of the Lord your God that I give you" (Deuteronomy 4:2 NIV).

17

Here and Hereafter

To my surprise, I'm still not ready to wind all this up with a humdinger how-to-do-it chapter. There are a few more things that need to be said which include a further humbling of your servant Hal Hill. I have to take back something I've said over and over again, lambasting folks who've talked about pie-in-the-sky-by-and-by. Looking down my shiny nose at them, I've implied they were all wet—that we could have the full benefits of heaven's best while we were still walking around on Planet Earth.

That, my friends, hasn't been my total experience—or yours—because it simply isn't scriptural, no matter who says it.

I'm leaving the rest of this page blank to give you a chance to recover your Adam's apple in case you swallowed it. And to give me a chance to look in the mirror and see if I'm still here. It was hard to say that. But I needed to.

Have you forgiven me for misleading you for so long? Let's be realistic for a minute—scriptural, too.

At this point, let's find out how God's idea of heaven's best checks with our own. In most cases, there's a vast difference between our viewpoints. God's definition of heaven's best has to do with eternal values and long-range results; ours, with our immediate needs, whimsies, or lusts of the flesh. That's why seeking wisdom from above is point number one in looking for heaven's best in each happening of life on Planet Earth. Then let's go on to some of the factors entering into situations where heaven's best may not be what we imagined or hoped for.

1. Having in mind the single-eye-on-God principle of the Bible, anything that competes with God for our attention, affections, or worship is less than heaven's best in God's sight. Yes, even diligent Bibly study, prayer at precisely the same hour each day, and dedicated church activities could stand in the way of our usefulness in God's perfect plan for our lives.

2. Knowing from God's Word that He has us in training down here for more successful functioning up there, we could find that what we consider heaven's best might, in God's sight, be sin. Does that jolt your theology? Try this verse on for size: "Whatsoever is not of faith is sin" (Romans 14:23).

A quick and easy prayer-answering system requiring no faith on our part robs us of faith growth and robs God of glory.

3. Whatever glorifies God, blesses others, and builds our faith in Him, without becoming a false God, could be considered heaven's best on any particular occasion. But not as a doctrine to be slapped on one another as a permanent formula for instant success. Each living experience contains elements known only to God, so that heaven's best for me

today may be drastically different from heaven's best for me tomorrow. And for you, the combination of circumstances God sees at work in your life may require totally different treatment from His work in me.

4. If heaven's best for me today is a two-seater donkey, maybe a three-seater Mercedes would become an object of worship in my life at my stage of spiritual growth. God in His infinite wisdom and mercy may withhold, for the present, such gifts or blessings until a time when they would not become a false God to me. But maybe you can handle those hundreds of horses under the hood today, without their becoming false idols in your life. That's God's business. Only He knows that last remaining fact about all of His King's kids, and He suits our prayer answers to our needs and not our wants. And don't overlook the fullness-of-time factor. God never does.

5. If my "perfect record" of self-achievement causes me to adversely judge your less-than-perfect performance record, then my phony self-image must be exploded in order to make way for heaven's best in my life. Maybe that's why my religious status symbol of many years endurance, my "happily married" phony front, had to dissolve right before your very eyes in order to jolt this Pharisee from his self-righteous throne of my former attitude of "holier than thou" because "your marriage is broken and mine is not, you dirty old sinner. Therefore I'm saintlier than you are." God has forgiven me, and you'll have to also, for my misleading you into thinking I had heaven's very best under all conditions, while I conveniently left out lots of details which you haven't known about until now.

Heaven's best in our lives may be still awaiting our willingness to let go of second best, which although acceptable to us may miss by far what God has in mind for us, maybe even years down the road when the prophecy "will surely come to pass."

So when I assumed that an unbroken marriage was heaven's best in my own life, and tended to translate that into a doctrine for everyone around me, God had to blow that one away once and for all.

"Whoa!" someone shrieks. "Brother Hill is saying that God is a marriage wrecker!" No such thing. Just calm down, take a deep breath, and listen to some of the details. When I asked Jesus to take charge of my life and affairs back in 1954, He took me at my word, knowing it was God working in me both to will and to do of His good pleasure (Philippians 2:13). Knowing all the facts in my life and affairs which might stand in the way of working out His perfect plan for my individual life, He made provision for certain roadblock removal by permitting certain events to take place which at the time seemed horrendous and completely contrary to my idea of what He could do to make me usable in His scheme. Having delivered me from alcoholism, He knew He could entrust the lives of other hurting alcoholics to my care for ministering His love and compassion, as He had ministered them to me through others of like affliction in Alcoholics Anonymous.

But another, and probably equally great, segment of humanity also needed understanding, compassion, and ministry which I was not equipped to give—the great multitudes of hurting people involved in the tragic circumstances of broken marriages. How could I, with my supercilious, self-righteous attitude toward those hurting little ones, ever be expected to help heal their hurts, except through understanding love which comes through the experience of a blown marriage? And so it came, in a way which literally transported me into the kingdom of God, removed a false god from my life, namely, an already tottering marriage, which was a real roadblock to total usefulness in God's plans for many lives. I have since been privileged to minister to such lives through the understanding which comes only through experience. Thus being fitted into God's ministry of reconciliation (2 Corinthians 5:18) makes any price cheap, considering the eternal values involved.

When God's in charge, no amount of prayer will sway Him from His perfect will in our lives, just as much prayer over the years has done nothing toward restoring my own fractured marriage. Forgive me for misleading you into thinking it had.

True, Ruth and I reside at the same street number and share the same telephone, as do lots of other condo dwellers. But I have understanding about loneliness, heartache, and all the rest, and no longer judge you when you hurt in these areas. Now I, too, understand that Jesus handles such tragedies just right. Only trust Him for the final results. I am.

Heaven's best? You name it. God's in charge here.

If we're going to live with Him in eternity, the promises of God have to have eternal ramifications. If we ignore that fact and squeeze out the eternal in our efforts to force all His promises into our earthly years—which are like an eye blink compared to the rest of it—we may shortchange ourselves.

The Bible says we will be like Him when we see Him as He is (1 John 3:2), not before. For now, it seems we're being changed into His likeness gradually, from one degree of glory to another, as we look on Him. Then, when we see Him face to face, something will happen in the twinkling of an eye. In the same way, perhaps, some healing is for now—to serve God's own purposes, among them to bring men to faith—but total wholeness, which is far more than healing, may be saved for the hereafter. Total wholeness now would probably blow all our fuses—our finite minds couldn't handle it. It's too powerful for these earthen vessels of ours.

Meanwhile, because of advances in medical science, we're getting more and more sneak previews of what the next installment of eternal life will be like—with Jesus and without Him. My own heart attacks (read all about them in *How to Be a Winner*) gave me a sneak preview of life hereafter—*with* Him. I liked what I saw. Since King's kids are headed for life everlasting with Jesus, everything good that God has for them doesn't have to happen in the here and now. Some of the good things may be saved for later. Are there scriptural indications that this is so? Plenty of them! Chances are, none of them are underlined in your Bible yet, because most of us faith teachers have pretended they didn't exist.

Do you have your pencil in hand? Maybe you'd better use ink for this exercise. Here we go:

In a section headed "Future Glory" in the New International Version, Paul wrote these words to the Romans (brackets are mine):

> I consider that our present sufferings are not worth comparing with the glory that will be revealed in us. [He didn't say *when* it would be revealed, but it's plain from the verses that follow that it hasn't happened yet.] The creation waits in eager expectation for the sons of God to be revealed. For the creation was subject to frustration, not by its own choice, but by the will of the one who subjected it, in hope that the creation itself will be liberated from its bondage to decay and brought into the glorious freedom of the children of God. [Is there still decay going on around you? Of course! If you don't believe it, lift the lid of your garbage can! Apparently creation isn't yet fully liberated.]
>
> We know that the whole creation has been groaning as in the pains of childbirth right up to the present time. Not only so, but we ourselves, who have the firstfruits of the Spirit [*Firstfruits?* Does that mean there will be more somewhere later? Sounds like it to me!], groan inwardly as we wait eagerly for our adoption as sons, the redemption of our bodies. [Here the Amplified Bible clarifies with

"the redemption of our bodies (from sensuality and the grave)," and I have to confess that hasn't happened to me yet. Sounds again as though there's something yet to come.]

Romans 8:18–23 NIV

Let's look at another one, this time from Paul's letter to the Philippians (1:6 NIV): ". . . being confident of this, that he who began a good work in you will carry it on to completion until the day of Christ Jesus." What does that mean? The Amplified Bible gives this explanation of the phrase "until the day of Christ Jesus," based on the fuller meaning of the Greek words than our English vocabulary conveys: "right up to the time of His return." It keeps on sounding like something good is going to happen later that hasn't already appeared, doesn't it.

Look at this from Paul's second letter to the Thessalonians. It gives us some clues about what the day of the Lord is all about, so you can know whether or not it has happened yet:

God is just: He will pay back trouble to those who trouble you and give relief to you who are troubled, and to us as well. [When? Listen to this!] This will happen when the Lord Jesus is revealed from heaven in blazing fire with his powerful angels. He will punish those who do not know God and do not obey the gospel of our Lord Jesus . . . on the day he comes to be glorified in his holy people and to be marveled at among all those who have believed.

2 Thessalonians 1:6–8, 10 NIV

And here's more: "No eye has seen, nor ear has heard, no mind has conceived what God has prepared for those who love him" (1 Corinthians 2:9 NIV).

"You can now hope for a perfect inheritance beyond the

reach of change and decay, reserved in Heaven for you" (1 Peter 1:4 PHILLIPS), or as the Today's English Version paraphrase has it, "And so we look forward to possessing the rich blessings that God keeps for his people. He keeps them for you in heaven, where they cannot decay or spoil or fade away."

"Then will the eyes of the blind be opened and the ears of the deaf unstopped. Then will the lame leap like a deer, and the tongue of the dumb shout for joy" (Isaiah 35:5, 6 NIV).

Want some further verses indicating there is something better later that we don't have yet?

"Who gave himself for our sins, that he might deliver us from this present evil world" (Galatians 1:4). "We know [positively] that we are of God, and the whole world [around us] is under the power of the evil one" (1 John 5:19 AMPLIFIED). "For it was not to angels that God subjected the habitable world of the future, of which we are speaking" (Hebrews 2:5 AMPLIFIED).

"If only for this life we have hope in Christ, we are to be pitied more than all men" (1 Corinthians 15:19 NIV).

Well, there are many more, but here's the clincher:

> And I saw a new heaven and a new earth: for the first heaven and the first earth were passed away; and there was no more sea. And I John saw the holy city, new Jerusalem, coming down from God out of heaven, prepared as a bride adorned for her husband. And I heard a great voice out of heaven saying, Behold, the tabernacle of God is with men, and he will dwell with them, and they shall be his people, and God himself shall be with them, and be their God. And God shall wipe away all tears from their eyes; and there shall be no more death, neither sorrow, nor crying, neither shall there be any more pain; for the former things are passed away.

Revelation 21:1–4

Who said that God has to finish His work with us in this dimension we call Planet Earth? Who said this is the final testing ground? I don't know who it was, but whoever he was, these verses indicate he was all wet.

I have good friends who have a deaf teenager. There have been plenty of prayers, and we know God may choose to hand her perfect ears any day now. Meanwhile, she's equipped with a pair of powerful hearing aids to keep her aware of what's going on around her. One day, as a matter of research, her mother asked her a loaded question:

"Considering all the things that have happened so far in your life, would you rather be deaf or hearing?"

The teenager thought for a minute before she answered. Then she said, "Deaf."

"Why?" her mother asked her.

More thought, then a shrug of the shoulders and this answer: "God made me."

In other words, God was in charge of that young lady's life from the beginning, and she sensed He must have had some special purpose in mind for making her exactly the way she was. That didn't mean there weren't huge disadvantages to deafness, just as there are huge disadvantages to Joni's wheelchair and Merrill Womach's scarred profile. But all things considered, if God seems to indicate that He has some reason for letting "tragedy" happen in the life of a particular person, and uses it to His glory, maybe we should join the "victims" in praising the Lord for whatever He gives them to go with, whether it looks good or bad to us. Meanwhile, the best hearing aids possible, the best special education, the most comfortable wheelchair, and whatever else the Lord provides to help them cope with life—they're all welcome. We're not to waste a lifetime fretting about all the apparently unanswered prayers in each case; we're to praise the Lord and go with what we've got, continuing to pray at every opportunity, to be anointed with oil, but making the best of daily life in the midst of it.

Scriptural? Of course!

Being content in whatever state we find ourselves, as Paul said he was, can't mean cursing the devil all day long because we lack in the present stage of our existence the wholeness God has stored up for us in the fullness of time, whether that happens to be on earth tomorrow, or later in the heavenly realm. If God chooses to give us a portion of our wholeness here, well and good. If He chooses to give only part of it, or none of it, He's the Potter who can do as He pleases. Meanwhile, He gives the grace to handle whatever imperfection remains.

What if He works an out-and-out miracle? The educated idiot boxes of those who choose not to believe can discount a miracle in a hurry, persuading themselves they imagined the whole thing. "I guess so-and-so wasn't as sick as we thought," folks can say, instead of praising God for His mercy. I've seen it happen.

But the witness of someone coping with imperfection and reflecting the love of God in the midst of it isn't so easily dismissed.

Look again at the pottery business. God says, "Is it any of your business if I make some pots for noble purposes—maybe to sing Handel's *Messiah*—and some for ignoble?" (You name here whatever is ignoble to you.) There is all kinds of work that needs to be done, and we're the tools He has with which to do it. It's important for me to recognize that His plan and purpose for me may not be the same as His plan and purpose for the man next door, so He has to give each of us a different set of equipment to accomplish it.

Maybe part of what He's trying to do with us here is to mold us and shape us to fit the space and activities in glory-land. He has to purify us from selfishness, or heaven won't work. There's no place to keep our unforgiveness there. We have to get rid of it on this plane—and our selfishness—so we can be ready to prefer the other fellow ahead of ourselves.

Is laying up treasures for yourself in heaven instead of on earth compatible with the concept of a Cadillac in every carport and an Olympic-sized swimming pool in every backyard, as some faith teachers have taught? Or with the Bible concept of setting affection on things above and not on things on earth? Whoa! Don't make a doctrine out of that, either, because it all depends on God's assignment for the particular person. Sometimes the Cadillac might be appropriate, and even *two* swimming pools. For someone else, a one-speed donkey and a small birdbath might constitute an extravagance. Always, it all depends. It's all up to God. We can't afford to criticize.

Before it's too late, I need to insert a disclaimer. This book isn't meant to lambast faith teachers—I praise God for them! And I'm even one of them. Jesus was interested in faith: "Will I find faith when I come?" He wanted to know (*see* Luke 18:8). But we need to make sure that our faith is in who He *is*—sovereign God who knows what He's doing—and not a God who can be manipulated to do *our* will.

If we refuse to make doctrines, and instead let each King's kid be led by the Spirit, we'll all have a chance to fit better into His plans. And we'll save gasoline by not taking so many guilt trips or sending others on equally nonproductive expeditions to fit into our ideas of what they ought to be doing.

Clearly, there will be a day when all that King's kids are yearning for now will be manifested. But that day isn't today. For now, we're stuck with making the best of things on a sin-cursed planet, under the rule of the prince of the power of the air (Ephesians 2:2), and we have to wrestle "against the despotisms, against the powers, against [the master spirits who are] the world rulers of this present darkness, against the spirit forces of wickedness in the heavenly (supernatural) sphere" (Ephesians 6:12 AMPLIFIED).

All that wrestling would be pretty impossible with ordinary weapons, but we're not limited to them. Through the gifts of the Spirit, God has made available armor to protect us against the enemy (you can read about the whole inventory in Ephesians 6) and a super weapon to use against him, the sword of the Spirit, which is the Word of God. (You can read how that works in Hebrews 4:12.) The sword of the Spirit isn't a weak, carnal weapon, but one that is "mighty through God to the pulling down of strong holds" (2 Corinthians 10:4).

With spiritual armor and spiritual weapons, we're all set to win the battle, if we will only fight it. Too often, folks give up and settle for second best, dreaming up a thousand reasons why the Bible way of handling these things won't work for them. We won't fault them for that, but we don't have to be ignorant of the spiritual gifts and settle for second best ourselves. We can take what God offers and use it. Then, and only then, we'll be in a position of "having done all," and can stand and see what God will do for us (Ephesians 6:13).

What's included in the "having done all"? A whole Manufacturer's Handbook full of directions—all scriptural, all able to work together for good, all highly recommended, all totally impossible in our own strength. But one of the best parts of the Good News is that we don't have to do anything in our own strength anymore. When Jesus said, "If you love me, you *will* keep my commandments" (John 14:15 RSV, my italics), He *had* to mean that He would keep them for us, in us.

Paul could have had something like that in mind when he wrote to the Galatians:

> In other words, through the Law I am dead to the Law, so that now I can live for God. I have been crucified with Christ, and I live now not with my own life but with the life of Christ who lives in me. *The life I now live in my body I live by believing* [Amplified says that *believing,* in the sense of *having faith,* means "leaning ... the entire human personality on Him in absolute trust and confidence in His power, wisdom and goodness" (Colossians 2:5)] ... *in the God and Christ who loved me and* who sacrificed himself for my sake.
>
> Galatians 2:19, 20 JERUSALEM and BECK,
> italicized portions only

With the life of Christ living in us, being our wisdom, righteousness, sanctification, and redemption (1 Corinthians 1:30), what more could we ask? How can we fail? There's no way, as long as we depend on Him.

PRINCIPLE: " 'What are the works God wants us to do?' they asked him. Jesus answered, 'This is the work God wants you to do: believe in the one he sent' " (*see* John 6:28 NEB, 29 TEV).

18

How to Do It

We're finally here, at the windup, to discuss how to go about living this life of King's kids under construction on a sin-cursed planet so as to get the best possible results, knowing that heaven is saved for later, and that things earthside might be less than perfect a good bit of the time. We've looked at a lot of things that might have upset the theologies by which we operated in the past, and we've made no doctrines but observed a few principles along the way.

What, then, do all these experiences, observations, purposes, and principles mean in relation to our walk through this life as King's kids? Are there any conclusions we can draw—without inventing doctrines that will trip us up? Should we quit trying because we see that folks don't always seem to succeed—as we judge success? Should we stop praying because our prayers sometimes seem to fail—as folks figure failure?

Or should we try harder than ever, in every way the Manufacturer recommends, to make this life work for the best possible results in the here-and-now as well as in the hereafter?

Brother Paul seems to have chosen the latter course, and maybe we, as finite creatures like him, could afford to take a look at what he did. Here's how he expressed his intentions about his future actions at one point:

I do not claim that I have already succeeded or have already become perfect. [Does that feel familiar?] I keep striving to win the prize for which Christ Jesus has already won me to himself. ... I ... forget what is behind me and do my best to reach what is ahead. So I run straight toward the goal in order to win the prize, which is God's call through Christ Jesus to the life above.

                                   Philippians 3:12–14 TEV

What Paul said there is so plain that even I can understand it. God had called him, as He has called you and me, to head toward a very special kind of life that will last forever. On Planet Earth, we don't see any perfect examples of that kind of life, but we will ourselves *be* examples when we see Jesus as He really is (1 John 3:2). And the truth that Jesus is (John 8:32) just might be something we could take for our guide while we are still earthbound.

Paul was apparently talking along the same lines when he wrote this advice to Timothy: "Do your best to present yourself to God as one approved, a workman who does not need to be ashamed and who correctly handles the word of truth" (2 Timothy 2:15 NIV).

Notice that business about "truth" in this passage, too? It kind of stood out to me, and I think he's *not* talking about the doctrines of men—how about you?

Paul mentioned that truth business again when he wrote to the Ephesians and warned them of the tendency of the educated idiot box to be swayed by every doctrine that comes along. "Rather," he said, "let our lives lovingly express truth in all things—speaking truly, dealing truly, living truly" (Ephesians 4:15 AMPLIFIED).

Kind of a tall order, isn't it?

Again, in the sixth chapter, after he had written about the best basis for people-to-people relationships, he concluded, "Therefore put on God's complete armor, that you may be able to resist and stand your ground on the evil day ... and having done all ... to stand [firmly in your place]. Stand therefore—hold your ground—having tightened the belt of truth around your loins ..." (Ephesians 6:13, 14 AMPLI-FIED).

There it is again—that word *truth*—in a context that reminds me of the verse where it is written, "Sanctify them—purify, consecrate, separate them for Yourself, make them holy—by the Truth. Your Word is Truth" (John 17:17 AM-PLIFIED).

When Paul said "stand," I knew he didn't mean we were to stand and do nothing, because in another place, after telling the Philippians they should have the same attitude Christ had, he said they were to "work out" their salvation. One translation says it this way: "... with reverence and awe *keep on working* clear down to the finishing point of your salvation ... for it is God Himself who is at work in you to help you desire it as well as do it" (Philippians 2:12, 13 WILLIAMS, my italics).

Finally, he said to them that they should keep on thinking about the good things, not just as an interesting mental exercise, but in order to "practice what you have learned and received and heard and seen in me, and model your way of living on it ..." (Philippians 4:9 AMPLIFIED). Why should they do all this? For a very good reason: "... then the God who gives us peace will be with you" (Philippians 4:9 WIL-LIAMS). Something worth aiming at, wouldn't you agree?

Well, the more I read of these Scriptures telling me in one way or another to keep on living by all the truth I had learned, the more blessed I got. But I couldn't keep on just sloshing around in the Scriptures indefinitely. I had a deadline to meet if this book was ever going to be published, and I had to decide on some approach—not a doctrine, remember—to get all the necessary words down on paper.

"But there's just no way, in the pages of a small book, to cover all the truth that's in God's Word!" I complained.

It presented me with a sort of dilemma.

One night I went to bed thinking about all these things and how to incorporate them in a book the size of this one. All during the night, the Lord kept waking me up, impressing me with an inquiring message: "Check your ingredients. Have you included everything needful? Have you left out everything that won't be helpful to the finished product?"

It made me feel as if I were baking a cake or checking a cockpit prior to takeoff. So, being a scientifically systematic sort of person, I began a rundown, tackling it in alphabetical order, the way we used to recite the forty-eight states of the union with their capitals and largest cities when I was a kid. We all had to memorize how many states began with an *A*, how many with a *B*, and so on through the alphabet.

Well, I didn't have a memorized list of the *ABC*s of King's kid living at my fingertips, but as I thought my way down the alphabet, God had twenty-six opportunities to bring to my remembrance particular Scriptures.

It was so good thinking about them that later I got together with a concordance to dig up some more. Believe it or not, by the time I reached *Z* (that's for being *zealous* for God, and being *zealous* of spiritual gifts), I had enough treasures to fill thirty-three pages! And I'd barely scratched the surface.

"Whoa!" my editor hollered when I gave the alphabet to him. "There's not room for all that in a book this size. You'll have to cut it out and save it for another book, later."

But what I had begun to envision as *ABCs for King's Kids in Training* wouldn't wait. A still small voice seemed to say, *Hill, you could simply have the ABCs printed as a separate pamphlet you could send to anybody who wants one.* That struck me as a perfect idea. And so, if you'll send me a self-addressed, stamped envelope with *ABC* written in the lower left corner, I'll let you know how you can get your copy right away. My address is at the end of chapter one, remember.

Meanwhile, you can begin to compile a list for yourself. Get a concordance, as many translations of the Bible as you can find (you might choose to limit yourself to the New Testament to make it easier), and sit down for a real treasure hunt, digging out the particulars of the "all" included in the "having done all, to stand" of Ephesians 6:13.

Here's a tiny sampling to start you off:

A is for *abiding* in Him and letting His Word *abide* in me. . . . (I had more than a page full of *A*s!)

B is for *believing* on Him, *being* confident that the One who has *begun* a good work in me will *bring* it to completion, making manifest in my life all the *be-attitudes* that spell *blessedness* for those who are *born again* of incorruptible seed.

C is for *coming* unto Him, who invites all who are loaded down with the *cares* of the world to *cast* their *cares* on Him, because He *cares* for them.

Have you got the hang of it? *A* through *Z*, *alpha* through *omega* (the first and last letters of the Greek alphabet)—every single letter has something that can remind me of Jesus and His plan for best results for King's kids in the Planet Earth installment of their adventures in eternal life. The Manufacturer's Handbook is the right place to look for the whole story of how things happen when we let God be in charge of our comings and goings.

Happy hunting! Report back to me in sixty days so I'll know the progress you are making. And if you come up with any new goodies to add to my list, send them along. Who knows? They might be cranked into the next manuscript that's always simmering on the back burner. King's kids never tire of looking into the Manufacturer's Handbook and learning more about His plans for them.

PRINCIPLE: "Every Scripture is God-breathed—given by His inspiration—and profitable for instruction, for reproof and conviction of sin, for correction of error and discipline in obedience, and for training in righteousness [that is, in holy living, in conformity to God's will in thought, purpose and action], So that the man of God may be complete and proficient, well-fitted and thoroughly equipped for every good work" (2 Timothy 3:16, 17 AMPLIFIED).

19

Questions, Anyone?

Questions, anyone? I seem to detect among my readers some unsettled eyebrows, as if they're still not perfectly satisfied with my satisfaction—you could even call it delight—that God's in charge here, whether I get my way or not. I hate to leave such folks discontented, so I'm winding this up with one more chapter to answer some burning questions that have been thrown at me by recent audiences in my getting about the country. Maybe some of the questions are the same as yours. If not, feel free to drop me a line at the King's Kids Korner, at the address listed at the end of chapter 1, and I'll see if I can answer your questions, too.

But here goes with what I've got already:

Q: Where does trouble come from?
A: I dunno. What we call "trouble" seems to come from lots of places. God doesn't give us a simple answer that settles it once and for all in His Manufacturer's Handbook, and so I can't give you one either. But from what I read in its pages, I see several possibilities. Want to hear them?

Some of the things or events that we call "trouble" may be the chastening of the Lord, designed to separate us from something second best. Other bits of trouble may be obstructions sent by the devil but used by God to turn our faith into pure gold. Or, as happens in many cases, trouble may be the natural cause-and-effect happenings of an orderly universe, resulting from the everyday poorly planned or badly executed behavior patterns of our I-can-do-it-myself-my-way human nature. One of the clearest illustrations I can think of for this origin of catastrophe is that of the man who jumps off a five-story building and winds up with a cracked cranium. He hasn't broken the law of gravity, he has only proved that it works.

A further possibility is that trouble could come from persecution for His name's sake, giving us a cross to bear which literally crosses out all our self-effort tendencies in favor of surrendering it all to Him and letting Him be completely in charge of our life and affairs. In some of these things called trouble, I see a spiritual cause-and-effect process in operation, in which Jesus seems to be saying, "If I'm willing to work within your limitations, why aren't you?"

The important thing to remember is that wherever it comes from, God can work it out for good for us if we let Him. Never forget, Romans 8:28 still works.

Q: Why do bad things happen to God's people?
A: Again, the Manufacturer's Handbook doesn't give one answer for all inquirers. The thing that seems most relevant to me here is that God is preparing us to rule and reign with Him in eternity. Thus, His program for now might be designed to make us ready for that assignment over yonder, not to settle a happily-ever-after on us now (which is only an eye blink compared to the rest of it). Some of the eternal promises from the God who can't lie may be set up for fulfillment in some other part of eternity than the three score years and ten, give or take a few, in which we inhabit Planet Earth.

According to Isaiah 35:5, 6, we won't need wheelchairs or hearing aids or contact lenses in heaven. The implication, as I read it, is that we might need a few of those things here.

We'll be needing crutches, too, if they happen to be part of the essential equipment for putting us in a position to win an orthopedic surgeon to the Lord, or to reach someone so shattered by useless limbs that he won't be able to "hear" our testimony unless it's obvious to him that we know how he feels because we're in the same predicament ourselves. I'm not giving that as doctrine, just as one way a fellow could look at such things.

Job's friends had a theology that said bad things happened to him because he had been a disappointment to God in some way, but God seems to have vindicated Job and straightened out their bad theology in the process. Whatever "bad" happens to God's people here, He seems quite able to reward them for faithfulness here or hereafter.

Did you ever stop to think that, the way earthlings are constituted, we'd have died of boredom a thousand years ago if God had given us a life that was all sunshine, never a flat tire or a mortgage due, never an opportunity to hold our breath in suspense or to use crutches, never anything major or minor that the world would call "bad"? If you've never stopped to think about it, try it for a minute with me.

A flat tire on a bicycle might not look like something good, but when it turns into an occasion for getting better acquainted with the only family in the neighborhood that has a tire pump, we can be almost glad it happened. Jesus told us to love one another—that's how we'll have the most fun in life—and if it wasn't for our need for one another, we wouldn't even know one another yet, much less be loving. Some of our getting acquainted—a whole lot of it—is triggered by calamity of one sort or another. You get to know the druggist because you need some medicine. You get to know a barber and a tailor because of your own inadequacies in the scissoring and sewing departments. You get to know a mechanic because something goes wrong with the motor of your car. You get to know a tree surgeon because lightning strikes a landmark. Tribulations seem to increase our interrelatedness and so increase our opportunities to love, which is what the bottom line of our existence is all about.

Q: How come some prayers seem to be answered and some don't?
A: Assuming you've met *all* the requirements for prayer as they are laid out in the Manufacturer's Handbook—asking in faith, nothing wavering, believing you receive what you ask for, forgiving anyone you've held a resentment against, speaking the words of faith aloud, getting two or three to agree with you about the concern in your prayer, making sure you are abiding in Him and He is abiding in you, making sure your prayer is in line with God's will, not praying selfishly for something you expect to consume on your own lusts, making your requests with thanksgiving, letting the Spirit pray through you when you don't know how to pray as you ought, coming to Him as His child, cleansing yourself of all sin, being humble and patient, and all the rest of it—

Pause here to come up for air while I say that if you haven't done *all*, it's not fair to ask why God hasn't answered your prayers. The fact of the matter is, He answers many prayers when we haven't met all the requirements at all—or even pretended to. But such is the mercy of God that He answers anyway.

But if you have met all the requirements and have no answer (I'm assuming you've been patient to wait as long as the situation requires), then there can be several other reasons your prayers aren't answered.

One important reason involves the free will of other people. Suppose, for instance, that someone has robbed you, and you pray for God to send the thief back to restore your property to you. If the thief doesn't choose to do it, you're stuck. God won't violate his personal freedom.

Another important reason seems to involve the faith—or lack of it—of other people. The Manufacturer's Handbook says that Jesus could do no mighty works in a certain place because of the unbelief of the people. I've seen that happen.

Years ago, Dr. Sam Shoemaker had a massive heart attack. As he lay dying in a Baltimore hospital, his teenage daughter, Nicki, telephoned me to see if I would go and help her pray for her daddy. Meanwhile, word had gone out to the ecclesiastical world that this great Episcopal priest and man of God didn't have much hope of pulling through.

As Nicki and I walked through the corridors to his room, we saw dozens of priestly robes and collars, but no bottles of anointing oil, and no one said to us, "Let's pray for Sam." Instead, they seemed to be busy advising his widow-to-be what to do after the funeral was over.

Did the solid wall of unbelief cause Sam to die? I don't know—we're still not making theologies, remember?—but it couldn't have helped Nicki's prayers and mine very much as we knelt beside Sam's bed and praised the Lord that at least we could act like believers while others seemed ready to get on with the funeral so they could go back home. I'm not saying their apparent attitude caused Sam to die, but that's the attitude that won the day.

What would have happened if we had all joined hands and hearts in one accord in a positive direction? I can't say. We never had a chance to find out.

A third reason our prayers might not be answered in the way we want them to be, after we have met all the scriptural requirements, is that sometimes God has a plan that is very different—and better—than anything our finite minds could figure out. Presuming to know what God is doing in the life of another person is treading on thin ice. There's an interest-

ing case of this in the last chapter of John. The Manufacturer's Handbook doesn't give a name to the malady, but I
call it "nose and mouth disease" and find it's pretty preva-
lent wherever King's kids gather.

In the Bible case, Peter was walking along with Jesus and
could have enjoyed His exclusive attention. But he had to
spoil it, as King's kids under construction are apt to do, by
getting nosy about Jesus' plans for the other fellow, in this
case, John.

"What about him?" Peter wanted to know as soon as
Jesus had given him his assignment in the sheep-feeding department.

Jesus answered far more politely than I might have done
under similar circumstances, naturally, but the sense of the
translation is, "None of your business, Pete. You keep your
nose out of it and just follow Me."

As I look at it, the plan of Jesus for each one of us is a
highly unique, individual plan. Because of the one-of-a-kind
plans He dishes out, He might let me get away with something that would be off limits for everyone else, depending
on His plan for me. On the other hand, He might require me
to toe the mark about something where you could be scot-
free. He's in charge here. Our noses are best kept in our own
business, but unfortunately, nose and mouth disease is almost epidemic among folks who ought to know better.

A fourth reason? Sometimes, instead of having done all,
we have done nothing at all and still expect prayer answers
to come tumbling down from heaven. Apparently this happens with more frequency than you might imagine, because
God included an admonition about it in the letter He wrote
through James. Did you notice what he had to say about
unanswered prayer? Look at it: ". . . ye have not, because ye
ask not. Ye ask, and receive not, because ye ask amiss, that
ye may consume it upon your lusts" (James 4:2, 3). If King

James doesn't put it plainly enough, try the Living Bible: ". . . the reason you don't have what you want is that you don't ask God for it. And even when you do ask you don't get it because your whole aim is wrong—you want only what will give *you* pleasure."

Pretty plain, I'd say. Sometimes we don't get what we want because we don't ask God for it; at other times we do ask but we ask with motives that are selfish. God can clean us of both kinds of defects if we ask Him to do it, and *then* we'll be in line to fulfill the requirement, ". . . having done all, stand" (Ephesians 6:13). "Having done all" involves quite a few things—you can read the whole Book of Ephesians for yourself to see what "all" involves. Then, when we have done all that, we can stand, and trust the outcome to God. It's not a do-nothing sort of passivity that accepts everything in the fatalistic, weak-Christianity way that sighs, "Oh, it's my cross to bear," but an activity that cooperates with what God wants to do every step of the way.

Jesus leads me to believe that often I have not because I ask not, indicating that He sorely wants to come through in all areas of my human need if I will just give Him a channel through which He can work. If I back off as far as possible into a crazy theology that says what I want is impossible, I come up with sure defeat when just one more little request to heaven might have produced a miracle God had prepared for me.

People have become pretty proficient in deciding what God can no longer do, but they're wrong just the same. Aren't you glad? I am.

It needs to be said that probably every doctrine of man has a sliver of truth—just enough to deceive us—but only God has it all. When we let Him be in charge, we can accept the fact that He always knows something we don't know, and that He is always eager to work in each of our lives, at any moment, but has to be subject to our willingness to accept Him in His role and under His conditions, not ours. Often there is a price we have to pay, such as willingness to "forsake all," and let Him do it—His way. That's what I've found to work best for me.

Q: Does God ever send "bad" things?
A: Did you ever hear of the plagues of Egypt? Where did they come from? If you've forgotten, refresh your memory with Exodus 7-12. 'Nuff said.

Q: Oh, but that's Old Testament stuff, Brother Hill, before the writers of the Bible knew what God was really like! He doesn't send bad things under the New Covenant—does He?
A: Maybe we need a little clarification here of what we mean by "bad" before an answer will have much relevance. To our limited minds, anything is "bad" that we don't like, right? To God's mind, what is bad? I don't know; He never told me. But look at what I find:

In Matthew 18, Jesus tells the story of the unforgiving fellowservant, whose master "delivered him to the tormentors" until he paid all he owed (verse 34). Then Jesus said, in effect, "That's what My heavenly Father will do to you, if you don't forgive everybody" (*see* verse 35). Who are the tormentors? The Manufacturer doesn't say, but in my own case once, it seemed I was turned over to the tortures of arthritis until I went and made things right with our family physician. (You can read all about it in chapter 28 of *How to Live Like a King's Kid*.) Maybe some other tormentors have been turned loose on you so you'll get in line with God's best for your life. If He chastens us and disciplines us, it's hard to believe we would consider it all a picnic, isn't it. But when the tormenting is finished, we can find it was worth it all, just to enter into His best for us.

Because God has given us free will to ignore His love if

we choose, sometimes our hardheadedness insists on real toughies before we'll surrender to His best for us. As I see it, no matter how hard He has to clobber us to get our attention, the act is love if it brings us to Him, which is the whole point of everything that happens on this planet. Anything, on the contrary, no matter how "good" it seems, that lets us go unpainfully on our merry way without bringing us to a knowledge of God, might *look* like loving-kindness but is really hatred and is so discerned when we look at the results in eternity.

Through Paul, writing to the Ephesians, God seems to put His stamp on everything—the good and the bad—that happens to us who belong to Him. Look at it—but don't make a doctrine of it:

> Moreover, because of what Christ has done we have become gifts to God that He delights in, for as part of God's sovereign plan we were chosen from the beginning to be his, and all things happen just as he decided long ago.
>
> Ephesians 1:11 TLB

And then comes the best part of the whole thing, the reason for it all: "God's purpose in this was that we should praise God and give glory to him . . ." (Ephesians 1:12 TLB).

I don't know whether that's good enough for you, but it's good enough for me. He's working everything together to get us all to praise Him. I'm ready to do it right now, aren't you?

A church bulletin crossed my desk a few days ago that summed all this up in a way worth remembering:

> Pity the poor unbeliever who, with all his fears and frustrations, attributes the conflicts that come into his life to be merely the arrangements of men who threaten to de-

stroy him. How different are the "Elishas" who know the living God and know that He has arranged our conflicts, adversities, and distresses "after the counsel of his own will" (Ephesians 1:11)!

God's purpose is to bring us into closer fellowship with Himself by developing our trust in His wisdom to perfect His plan for our lives. "Consider him that endured such contradiction of sinners against himself, lest ye be wearied and faint in your minds" (Hebrews 12:3). It is not necessary to understand God's reason for our trials, but it is of utmost importance that we remain faithful to Him.

I don't know where the church got the two paragraphs for its "Thought for Today," but I couldn't have said it better myself.

Q: Brother Hill, I agree with everything you say, but it seems there are too many different requirements for prayer in the Scriptures. How on earth can I ever do all I'm supposed to do to get a single prayer answered?
A: Now, that's what I call a good question. As a matter of fact, I checked it out with the Lord recently myself, and here's the analogy He gave me. If you're old enough, you'll understand it.

Do you remember the radio receivers of fifty years ago? They didn't have nice, convenient push buttons or clicky switches that got you the station frequency you wanted simply and accurately. Instead, they had three or more dials on the front of the radio, all of which had to be exactly tuned to the proper setting in order to tune in the program clearly or, in fact, at all.

When a fellow sat down to tune the separate circuits to the station he had in mind, he had to wait patiently during a silent warm-up period. The next thing that happened was a series of whistles and grunts, mixed with static, followed by more of the same as the several dials were manipulated to the numbers given on the instruction sheet.

Finally, after sometimes five minutes of holding your breath, straining your ears, and twiddling the dials with infinite precision, some form of intelligible program sometimes rewarded you for your troubles. It was iffy business at best, but we must have judged the results worth the trouble or we wouldn't have bothered.

What was happening down inside the set while we twiddled? Without knowing the scientific principles involved, the person tuning the set was lining up the receiving mechanism to correspond to the wavelength of the transmitting station. In marketing such radios, the manufacturer was saying to the user, "Either tune your set to our way of operating, or else go without results of the kind you desire." So we twisted and twiddled far into the night, without complaining, in order to pick up weak and often garbled radio programs. That was the best we had in those days.

With today's radios and television sets, the procedure is far simpler for us. We have only to push a button or click a switch in order to accomplish what took so much work in those early days. The principles are the same, but the manufacturer has simply combined all the dial functions into a single control so our part in the tuning process is practically effortless. We conform to the requirements of circuit tuning the modern way and seldom think about all the improved technology that has made it possible.

"But what's all that got to do with prayer?" my original questioner is hollering. Just hold your horses, I'm about to get to that.

When we pray using an intellectual approach, we try to "line up" all the dials and circuits to match our idea of the variables involved in a particular case. "Is it lack of faith in the patient, hidden sin in the pray-er, or what?" There are so many variables in the "circuit" which can hinder or block prayer results that our heads can go round and round like those old-time radio dials, hunting for alibis and reasons for our prayer failures.

But God has a better, or more "modern" streamlined way since His Holy Spirit came to be our Comforter. That way is through the gifts of the Spirit, nine in number, which God has provided so He can come through unrestricted, on His wavelength, corresponding each time to the particular conditions involved in the problem without the necessity for our going through all the iffy tuning business.

How does this work? One prayer—with the Spirit and with the understanding—for the healing of arthritis produced a word of knowledge that said, "Get rid of all sugar and white flour in your diet, and you'll soon be fit as a fiddle." If you were in the doctrine-making business, you might decide that all arthritics were to be healed in exactly that way, but you'd be wrong, as doctrine makers generally are.

The next prayer for the healing of an arthritic might produce the gift of knowledge that here is a patient who needs to go and forgive somebody. In the next case, the Spirit might give us discernment to see that a demon spirit was causing the locked joints. . . .

Looking unto Jesus, through the gifts of the Holy Spirit that He gives us to minister His grace to others, we can receive His wisdom, knowledge, discernment, gifts of healing, and all the rest, and so experience more positive prayer answers all around—without dial twiddling. In such cases, we get what we say, because God is speaking truth through us.

When God has "tuned our circuits," so to speak, through the gifts of the Holy Spirit tuning system, there are no "iffies" to worry about. All circuits are tuned by the Holy Spirit, and God is always glorified by the results. Furthermore, our puny weaknesses are bypassed in favor of His sovereign will. Then our words are literally His Word as we abide in Him and His Word abides in us. That spells victory in any language, and if things don't seem to go our way, we still acknowledge that God's in charge here, and He's going to work it all—the bad and the good—for our good, in the fullness of time.

(For easy-listening instructions on how to operate in the realm of the gifts of the Holy Spirit, send for the six-hour cassette album *Using the Gifts of the Spirit,* King's Kids' Korner, P.O. Box 8655, Baltimore, MD 21240.)

I'll await your further questions with eagerness. Meanwhile, let me sum it up again, to make sure we understand each other:

We live on a cursed planet, under cursed conditions. There are thorns and thistles in our gardens and a hope of Eden in our hearts. We live in the domain of Satan. He's the prince of this world, in rebellion against the soon-coming King. It's no secret that all kinds of bad things happen— even to King's kids—but they're all subject to redemption in the fullness of time. We're to pray about everything, to come into line, by His grace, with everything possible in His Word, and trust Him to bring us in line for the rest. Studying to show ourselves approved, we can get rid of all the roadblocks He reveals to us.

Having done all, we're to stand and see the salvation of the Lord. Sometimes He finishes the job here and now. But we don't always see the end of it earthside. There are some cases where the fullness of time just isn't going to happen until Jesus returns. Why not? We frankly and freely say, "We dunno, but God's in charge here."

As we live in the midst of imperfection, we see a lot of things we don't have to accept the way they are. Applying the gifts of the Spirit, we provide the channel for God to be God and make a difference. There are other areas where, pray as we may, a circumstance doesn't change. In such cases, the serenity prayer of Alcoholics Anonymous might be a good one: "God, grant me the serenity to accept the things I can't change, the courage to change the things I can, and the wisdom to know the difference."

Meanwhile, we have a hope in the hereafter for blessings we can't handle here. And we don't need to be put under condemnation by the doctrines of any man. In spite of what "they" say, in spite of what I have said in the past, the spiritual life is a life of uncertainty. Otherwise, such qualities as patience, endurance, perseverance, and faith would not be so strongly stressed throughout the Bible's teaching concerning the believer's trip on Planet Earth.

Be liberated, as I have been, by recent broadcasts in which I heard a great faith teacher demonstrate that there was more to the truth than what came from his mouth: "What you say is what you get! I haven't been sick for ten years!" he boomed week after week and month after month, making me feel guilty over a sore hangnail. Then one day the mellifluous (I've always wanted to use that word) voice was interrupted by quite audible sniffles and—horror of horrors!—a well-developed and powerfully explosive sneeze!

"Wow, Lord!" I exclaimed. "He's just like me—human, after all!"

I haven't heard that brother laying guilt trips on sneezers since that day, although he was still making me nervous about finances, claiming, "God has met my financial needs abundantly over the years simply because I always asked in faith, believing. If your finances are not in good condition, brother, it's just because you haven't believed hard enough."

You wouldn't have any idea how hard I squinched my muscles to believe for money with which to pay bills, money that was rightfully mine to expect from those who owed me large sums. When it didn't come, how guilty that brother made me feel.

And how liberated I was recently when I heard him begging the people to send in increased offerings to support the ministry that would be going off the air if they didn't hurry.

None of it is as simple as we have tried to make it in the past, wanting to formulate all the principles of God into one neat little pill that we could administer with guaranteed-perfect results to every aching heart. It was good to teach faith. We need to continue to teach it. But maybe the time has come for us to teach some other things, too, stirring some hope and love into the picture.

The bottom line? One day to hear Him say, "Well done, good and faithful servant. You have been faithful in a few things, now take charge of many" (*see* Matthew 25:23).

PRINCIPLE: Try Genesis 1:1 all the way through Revelation 22:20, 21: "In the beginning God created.... Even so, come, Lord Jesus. The grace of our Lord Jesus Christ be with you all. Amen."